CATS IN FACT AND FOLKLORE

The Moon

The Moon is like a big round cheese
That shines above the garden trees,
And like a cheese grows less each night,
As though some one had had a bite.

The Mouse delights to nibble cheese,
The Dog bites anything he sees—
But how could they bite off the Moon
Unless they went in a balloon?

And Human People, when they eat
They think it rude to bite their meat,
They use a Knife or Fork or Spoon:
Who is it then that bites the moon?

CATS

IN FACT AND FOLKLORE

VIRGINIA C. HOLMGREN

HOWELL
BOOK HOUSE

Howell Book House
A Simon & Schuster Macmillan Company
1633 Broadway
New York, N.Y. 10019

Library of Congress Cataloging-in-Publication Data
Holmgren, Virginia C.
    Cats in fact and folklore / Virginia C. Holmgren.
      p. cm.
    ISBN 0-87605-140-9
    1. Cats 2. Cats—Folklore 3. Cats—North America. I. Title
SF445.5.H65 1996
599.74"428—dc20   96–26566
                                   CIP

Manufactured in the United States of America
10 9 8 7 6 5 4 3 2 1

Book Design by Heather Kern

To all the wonderful cats, librarians, museum curators, photographers, family, friends, my ever-resourceful agent and a caring editor who have helped bring my long searching for the whole cat story to these pages.

CONTENTS

CATS IN FACT AND FOLKLORE

A SEARCH FOR BEGINNINGS

How cats first came in from the wild to become our loved and loving companions is a story that weaves its way through more than four thousand years and uncountable beginnings. On a search for facts to prove their taming, the questions to begin with are these: Where did taming start? When? Which wild species yielded first?

Like many another mystery of the ancient past, this one may never be solved completely. But persistent searching for proven records has yielded enough reliable answers to name African Wildcats first for steady taming and fix a date within only a few centuries of leeway.

EARLY CLUES

The first clue comes from anthropologists and archaeologists whose search for human beginnings found ancient catlike skeletons on all continents except Australia and Antarctica. So our search is narrowed by that much at least. On other continents the oldest catlike remains had been found buried in tar pits and bogs for something like forty million years. Some of those found in North America are older than any human remains yet found here. Some are larger than any tiger, lion or leopard now living. They are fascinating creatures, but they do not reveal where lap-size wildcats first became tame pets. Author Rudyard Kipling in his amusing *Just-So Stories* declares that First Cat tamed itself—just walked right into the cave where First Family lived and sweet-talked First Wife into granting First Cat forever-and-forever rights to a bowl of milk and a place by the fire.

1

AFRICAN WILDCAT, COPIED FROM A MURAL IN TOMB 3 (1950 B.C.) AT BENI HASAN IN 1890 BY FAMED EGYPTOLOGIST HOWARD CARTER, PUBLISHED IN 1893 BY P. E. NEWBERRY IN HIS BOOK, BENI HASAN.

Anyone who has watched one of today's stray cats make a similar appeal with a beguiling purr and pleading pose may agree with Kipling. But today's cats have a four-thousand-year history of sharing with humans. The first wildcats to be tamed were facing something completely new and would never have asked for milk or fireside. Milk for wild mammals is only for the unweaned young. Fire sends them into panicked flight. So we enjoy Kipling's story and look for facts elsewhere.

Anthropologists further our search with their discovery that clues to the ancient past can often be found by "digging" for old folk tales instead of skeletons. In early times when no written records were kept, tribal history was often remembered in stories. Almost every tribe had a storyteller, often called by a name that implied a link with magic. After all, some sort of supernatural interference often seemed the only reason why things happened as they did. Most storytellers were extremely clever at inventing plausible answers even when they had no idea of the real reason; not even the ghost of a hint. Such talent often saved them from disgrace, for the questions could come without warning, interrupting a tale with the whole village listening, and respect could be won—or lost—in an instant.

CAT TALES—IN STORY AND SONG

Stories that pleased were told again and again, passed from one storyteller to the next, remembered for centuries. Some of the best survived long enough to be put in writing, printed and published, including some about the first cats to become village pets.

One that may be the oldest still known was first told in some village in northeast Africa's lion country. There, one long-ago day, the village storyteller was pointing out the way mother cats teach their kittens how to catch mice, find a proper toilet place and otherwise behave themselves in approved cat fashion.

Suddenly someone interrupted. "But who taught the *first* mother cat?"

"Ahhh!" the storyteller might have exclaimed with a wise look, stalling for time to let the imagination simmer. "The *very* first? You really don't know?" The storyteller's pot of tricks must have come to full bubble and boil that day, for he soon launched into a horror tale of some long-gone day before the time when cats were at hand and hungry mice came raiding in droves.

"Oh, those terrible mice! How they swished and swarmed over the whole village. More and more! Into everything! Getting into every basket and bundle in every hut, gobbling down every scrap of food, clawing to bits anything that couldn't be eaten, dirtying everything they touched. Some even dared to nibble at the toes of the babies as they lay on their sleeping mats, setting them to screaming in pain and terror. Their mothers whirled to attack, stomping, yelling, slashing at the mice with whatever weapon came to hand till the mice finally retreated, disappearing into nearby brush and cranny. For the moment the mice were defeated, but the mothers knew they would return—still hungry—and that *something* had to be done."

The storyteller paused, gauging his listeners' response.

GULP. GRRUMMMFFF!!!

"What *could* be done?" he suddenly challenged them.

It was a clever trick to get an answer better than whatever the storyteller had in mind, but at first there was only silence. Then from somewhere in the circle came an old woman's creaky-crackly voice.

"Go to the lioness!"

All around the circle faces brightened. Why hadn't they thought of the lioness? Even their grand-mothers' grandmothers had known that the lioness was the

A LIONESS IN MINIATURE.

guardian of mothers and babies, for she was the wisest mother herself among all the creatures in Africa's veldt and jungle. The lion was king, but his mate was the one who held the family together, taught their young her own skills as huntress and provider.

"Of course, go to the lioness!" the storyteller repeated, as if that were intended all along. And since nothing more was coming from the creaky-crackly voice, the tale was finished as best as could be. Three women were chosen to ask for help, and the

STRIPES ARE STRIPES, BUT THE TIGER WASN'T RESPONSIBLE.

THE TAILS TELL THE TALES—AFRICAN WILDCATS WERE FIRST ANCESTORS OF TAMED WILDCATS.

lioness listened with concern, sharing their anger, but all the while knowing she could not ask her family to chase after anything so small and worthless as mice. If she took on such a task herself, she was certain to lose the respect she had gained through wisdom. Still, something had to be done.

Suddenly she nodded, knowing just how to help. With a low throat-clearing GRRRMMMPPPFFF! she neatly coughed up a piece of her lung onto a wide green leaf.

"Fold this leaf into a tidy packet," she told the puz-zled women. "Carry it carefully. Do not open the leaf till you have everyone in your village around you for witness. Then open it quickly and you will have the mouse-catcher you need."

They thanked her gratefully, did as she commanded, and when they finally opened the folded leaf there sat a little mottle furred creature that looked much like the lioness in miniature. Indeed, they told themselves in awed wonder, this little one would seem full lioness size to a mouse. As a murmur of approval went around the circle of watchers the little one opened its eyes wide, whole body alert as if it knew what was coming. And just then a mouse more daring than the rest came creeping out of its hiding place, heading straight for the nearest baby.

ZZZZIPPPP! The little furry one was after that mouse in a flash, caught it, gave it a shake and looked around for approval and . . .

Probably that first storyteller was looking around for approval, too, just then. And for years thereafter this tale would be told many times—with changes here and there, of course, for that's what happens to told-again tales as people forget something or have their own ideas. In one retelling that has survived the centuries, the lioness coughs up a piece of her liver instead of the lung. Perhaps this was a matter of forgetting. Either lung or liver added the same touch of magic listeners liked. Both stories also hid the fact that the poor narrator hadn't the least idea how the first tame cat mouser had come from the wild to be a village pet.

Another storyteller spins a quite different plot with Noah's Ark as the setting.

> *No cats appeared, for none existed. But all other animals went aboard, and once afloat all pledged to have no offspring till solid ground reappeared. All kept their word—except the mice. They increased as usual, litter upon litter, and the Ark was soon swarming with them. They scattered hither and yon, gnawing this, nibbling that, dirtying something else, till Noah (or some say Mrs. Noah) went to the lioness with desperate pleas for help. She agreed, and Noah took over, passing his hand above her bowed head once . . . twice . . . thrice . . . and . . . KER-CHOOOO!*
>
> *What a sneeze! The lioness bowed still lower and out came a tiny likeness of herself—the world's first cat, who was ready to fulfill the destiny of an expert mouser.*

This story was changed by later narrators, as usual. Some said this formidable sneeze came from a tiger—or tigress—*not* the lioness. Perhaps this began in Ararat where the Ark landed and tigers, not known in Africa, are the largest, most feared predators in the land. Perhaps someone thought the tigers' stripes made them a more logical ancestor of all cats with darker tabby markings—a pinch of realism in a pound of fantasy.

Today's clearer thinking suggests looking for wildcat ancestors with *both* a striped coat *and* a similar size. Three species make that match: European Wildcat, African Wildcat and Indian Desert Cat. All may have had the same unknown prehistoric ancestor. But the European species could not possibly have been involved in first taming because it has always been known as an animal that has never been tamed. Today, even newborn kittens rebel at human touch. Also, this European Wildcat has never lived in Africa, where the first tame cats were recorded. In addition it has a bushy, blunt-tipped tail, not the slim tapered tail of shorthaired housecats today and the two other small striped wild species.

As usual when fact and fantasy clash, a legend explains just how striped cats took the place of the plain-coated lioness. In Egypt, it went this way:

> *The all-powerful Sun god had three daughters to whom he granted the power to take the form of a lioness. One of them, the goddess Tefneut, quarreled bitterly with her father one day, and became so angry that she flew into a rage and stormed off in the form of a lioness. In full leonine fury she set out to ravish the land of Nubia on Egypt's southern border. The terrified Nubians begged the Sun god to take her away and never let her return.*
>
> *So he sent his most trusted emissary to solve the problem. Somehow the messenger coaxed Tefneut to keep the lioness form, but in a smaller size, with different fur and a gentle nature that all would admire. In this disguise, then, she returned with him to Egypt. There, in the temple at Bubastis where the lioness had for so long been worshiped as the guide for womankind, as a perfect mate and mother, she took the role of Bastet, the cat with a woman's body, and Egyptians began taming wildcats in her honor.*

Written records, bronze statues and amulets—not just legends—confirm the cat goddess was honored in Bubastis. Written records also bear witness that tamed wildcats were pets in Egyptian palaces and mansions at least by 2400 B.C. No record of tamed cats elsewhere has an earlier date proved with pictures and a written record of cats and humans together. Skeletons, or earlier sketches of cats alone, prove the animals were there, but do not prove that they were tamed. Half-tamed wildcats around farm villages may have come earlier and were tolerated for their

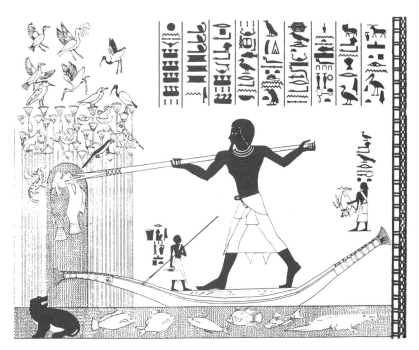

A WILDCAT IS AMONG THE PAPYRUS FLOWERS AT THE LEFT WITH
MONGOOSE AND GENET NEARBY WHILE MARSH BIRDS TRY TO
DEFEND THEIR EGGS AND HIPPOPOTAMUS AND CROCODILE WAIT
BELOW.

P.E.Newberry, *Beni Hasan.*

mousing skill, as were the less biddable mongoose and genet,
but were not fully adopted and cared for as cats would be in
Egyptian cities; and they were never linked to the gods.

SCIENCE STEPS IN

Two recently found claims of the first-ever cat are so ancient
that they are being accepted as proof wildcats were tamed
almost everywhere they roamed.

Archaeologists studying ruins on the island of Cyprus found
the jawbone of a long-dead wildcat in a cave occupied
by humans some seven thousand years ago. No other trace of
wildcats on Cyprus has ever been found. So some reporters have
concluded that this bone belonged to a living pet and must have
been brought from the nearby mainland of what is now Turkey.

This isn't impossible. But other theories are more logical. Just the bone—not a living animal—could have been brought as a sacred relic. Shamans in early times often valued certain bones, shells and other oddities for use in rituals, as part of their magic. Also, such a bone—even a whole skull or most of a skeleton—could have been washed ashore in stormy weather or caught in a fisherman's net, and saved as a curiosity or omen. A wildcat buried with a man in Middle Egypt about six thousand years ago comes closer to being proof of taming. A gazelle was buried at the man's feet too, and both animals could have been clan totems or food for the journey to the Afterworld or guides to that mysterious realm. A wildcat, able to see in the dark, could well have been a guide. Much as we want to accept the burial together as proof of taming, doubt remains. But taming would come with full proof and Egypt was where it happened.

How were these first pets tamed? The same way wild animals of any kind, anywhere, were tamed by primitive people. Hungry adult animals could be tempted to stay around with offerings of food, including mice they caught for themselves. Friendship came more often through adoption of abandoned kittens. Wildcats hunted near villages along the Nile where dense thickets gave shelter for dens.

A mother out hunting for food was all too often gulped down by a crocodile or trampled by an impatient hippopotamus. The kittens waited . . . waited . . . too hungry or too frightened to remember to keep silence, they whimpered. If luck was with them, they were heard by humans, not a predator, and rescued. Nature has programmed newborn birds and mammals to obey and follow a larger creature who takes them in charge. Usually it's the parent, but instinct doesn't always provide the ability to disobey a stranger if voice and touch are gentle. So a villager hearing the whimpers could easily take the kits home as playmates for the children—or as mousers. Allowed to roam freely, they often returned to the wild as soon as they were old enough to need a mate and might or might not return.

If too many cats stayed around, the surplus kittens might be sold at market, given away to friends or given to government officials when a favor was needed.

Three species of wildcats were eventually used in such exchanges. First and most often the African, as well as the very similar Indian Desert Cat and the larger Jungle Cat. The two latter species did not usually go as far south as the African, but they roamed eastward from Syria all the way to India. Perhaps they were aided on these eastbound journeys by caravan drivers eager to have companions—and trade goods that would sell quickly. Proof that all three were together at times in the temple at Bubastis is supplied by their mummified bodies found centuries later in the same burial ground.

Wild descendants of these three ancestral species are scarcer now, but still roam over much of the territory they knew in ancient times. Descendants of the first tamed pets are still seen in Egypt, too, and for nearly two thousand years the pharaohs were able to keep them there, forbidden to be taken from home boundaries. Then suddenly they seemed to be appearing almost everywhere at once, and so the story of the housecats' heritage goes from folk tales to written records.

CATS OF ANCIENT EGYPT

Ancient hunters in Egypt and the Near East all the way to Far East India's ocean shores all had soundalike names for whatever species of wildcats they knew. They sounded alike because they all imitated the cry that hunters heard when a cornered wildcat faced them with lips drawn back, and teeth bared for a defiant hissing challenge.

In Persia the name would one day be spelled *pusha*. In the Tamil speech of southern India, Malaysia and Ceylon it was *pusei*. In Sanskrit it was *puccha*. In Egypt, where symbols were written only for consonants and the vowels were left to memory, scribes used the symbols for *BSS* or *PSS*. Since tamed cats also hiss in defiant threat, the name served for them, too, in some places. But not in Egypt.

THE FIRST TAME CAT

According to long-held tradition, Egypt's first tamed cat to be remembered was a gift brought to the pharaoh Khafré who reigned from 2518 to 2493 B.C. One lingering rumor claimed the cat had come from Nubia—a point that might be linked to the legend of the goddess Tefneut who found her "cathood" there. Later, actual reports of wildcats and other wild pets from Nubia at least make the claim possible. Records of tamed cats document their presence before the end of Khafré's reign.

Believe it or not, there is also a bit of proof neatly ensconced in a sacred legend, that this first gift cat had supplied a new name that wild relatives had not known. Somebody there in Khafré's palace at Memphis (so the story goes) looked at the offered gift,

15

BIRDS AND BEASTS IN LANGUAGES AROUND THE WORLD HAVE BEEN NAMED BY THEIR VOICES. THE SPELLINGS DIDN'T ALWAYS MATCH,

calmly on leash there amid staring strangers, and jokingly tossed it a direct question: "Well, now, *who* are *you?*" And the cat calmly gave an equally direct reply: a polite, two-syllabled murmur. The joker gasped, turning to see if others had heard it too. They had! Gaping mouths and a stunned, staring look marked unbelieving amazement. All agog, they slipped off to spread the story. When asked for a name, the cat had told them. "M'yaow!" it had said. Plain as plain.

"Write it down," someone ordered a listening scribe. And because Egyptian writing used only consonants, he wrote MYW.

And so it was written in a sacred text of 2100 B.C. as Sia, Goddess of Wisdom, declared MYW as the cat's name *because*

M'YAOW

ME-YAT

PICTURES OR LETTERS—ONLY THE SOUND COUNTS.

that's what it had said. And the Sun god approved, taking MYW form on forays to defeat the serpent Demon of Darkness.

MEOW?—WHAT'S IN A NAME?

People the world over have been respelling MYW their own way ever since—*meow, miaou, miao, miau,* even *miauer.* The spelling used here has been deliberately chosen to be different and to keep the original consonants, in order to have a name belonging only to the tamed cats of pharaonic Egypt.

They deserve a unique name, for they are the ancestors of the first tame cats in Egypt and much of the rest of the world, as history will prove, and they were pets two thousand years before the word *cat* was ever seen in writing.

If m'yaows had become pets a few centuries earlier, their first written record would have been only the outline picture of a cat, for pictograms were how Egyptian writing began. By Khafré's reign, however, Egyptian scribes had devised sound symbols for each of more than twenty consonants. The symbols were still pictures, familiar objects easily recognized and so quickly memorized. But they held no meaning, only the sound arbitrarily assigned by the master scribes in the palace schools. For *M*—an owl. For *Y*—a reed leaf. For *W*—a baby quail chick. They were written in column, top to bottom, or in a line, right to left. **M Y W** was pronounced *m'yaow*.

To indicate a female, whether animal or human, a symbol that carried the sound of the letter *T* was added. It was a flat-based semicircle representing a loaf of bread, and to save space, or ease pronunciation, the *W* sign was often dropped when the *T* was added. So the word might be *m'yawat* or *m'yat*. By 2400 B.C. it was a name for baby girls as well as cats.

Scribes had trouble remembering that a vowel was needed between owl and leaf, so the owl was replaced by a milk jug. This was a new sign that was always followed by a vowel. Also, in case readers were still confused, most scribes added a guide sign. This was a stylized figure of a seated cat with the tail in an elegant S curve, sometimes half hidden behind the haunch. Asking if m'yaows ever sat on their tails like this before, curving them between leg and body, is pointless. Signs were officially stylized. No query about the tail shape and curve, either. A tapered tail held high is a m'yaow trademark. Almost all the surviving inscriptions use the milk jug, not the owl, and many use two leaves as reminder the sound is *Y* not *i* and the syllable is emphasized.

In these years, during each pharaoh's lifetime, a pyramid was built to hold his remains and all things needed for the Afterworld. Also included were images of the gods and goddesses he would meet there. On the walls, column after column of symbols told of their powers.

In time, these elaborate symbols were used only for writing in tombs and temples, so they are called *hieroglyphics*—sacred writing. For everyday use in business, general correspondence, records and books, even priests changed to symbols that became more and more simplified. At one stage *M* was just the double-curve brow line over the owl's eyes, *Y* only the leaf stem, *W* a curled-up wisp of fluff. By chance, this new *M* was borrowed for the alphabets that led to ours in English/American. So there's still an echo of a meow in every *M* or *m* we write.

This small but appealing link in the chain of cat heritage exists only because Egyptians believed firmly in the value of written records that could endure beyond human memory. They were not the first to use written symbols, but they put them to the fullest use in their time. The pharaohs themselves set an example by ordering numerous monuments and memorial panels in honor of their achievements and requiring scribes to record names and dates of each reign. Priests ordered illustrated inscriptions for the walls of tombs and temples, and pharaohs made doubly sure their own records would survive by ordering the construction of secret rooms to enclose their remains and treasures. Even the pyramids were looted in time, but thieves were usually after jewels and gold, not writing. Some tombs actually escaped discovery till the current century. More may still be found.

IT IS WRITTEN ON THE WALLS

The earliest royal pyramids were in the north near Memphis, home of the Sphinx. Later tombs were more often underground rooms and passages dug out of rocky hillsides at various places southward along the Nile. On the west bank across from the city of Thebes, at times the national capital, nobles and wealthy, high-ranking government officials had elaborate tombs prepared for themselves. They hired the best painters, sculptors, architects and craftsmen for every needed skill. Soon these experts also began choosing tomb sites around their village, adorning the walls as they once had those of the wealthy with storytelling scenes of the perfect ways of the Afterworld where all the pleasure known or hoped for in life would be theirs.

These murals, therefore, would be true indicators of the way people lived during that time, but all were touched with that Afterworld glow of perfection. Nothing would ever go wrong for the man whose mummified body would lie in the tomb while his spirit body found Afterworld bliss. In hunting scenes along the Nile's marshy thickets and ponds, the fowler is portrayed in perfect pose—throw-stick in one hand, decoy birds in the other, and always apparently successful. Success, too, for the fisherman with ready spear. A man might be alone or with family and pets—a dog, cat, perhaps genet or mongoose (both good mousers that were soon abandoned for a cat). And what were the cats up to? In some scenes they were hunting on their own in reedy thickets near the man's boat. In others they were faithfully at the hunter's side, reaching out to clutch whatever bird would be felled by a throw-stick's perfect aim.

Would the cat then claim the bird held in firm claws or surrender it to the hunter? The murals leave us guessing. In one, often presented as proof cats were trained retrievers, an orange-furred tabby has one bird in its teeth and a second held by the claws of both forefeet, with a third apparently safely between the hind feet. Just beyond a curved tail tip is a dazed-looking duck, perhaps stunned by a whack of that ever-moving tail.

Will the cat surrender them when the man holds out a hand? The mural has no sequel to provide an answer. But this scene, like the others, offers convincing proof of a m'yaow's cherished place on the cat history trail no matter whether the scene is factual or a dream-wish.

The trail would vanish abruptly for a time as Egypt was invaded by one army after another—all determined on full conquest. Persians came first in 525 B.C. and held on for two hundred years till the Greeks swept them out to rule for a three-century span, giving way in 30 B.C. to Rome. The Romans, who had seven long centuries of power, were ousted by Arabs in A.D. 642 as Egypt slowly became completely Arabic in language and customs, their own symbols forgotten—no one left who could write or read the messages on papyrus or painted walls.

The next invading conqueror was Napoleon, who arrived with his armies in 1798. Oddly, he was so fascinated by Egypt's lost history that he imported French scholars to search for whatever they could find. Not the scholars, but rather an alert soldier made the first discovery: a huge stone slab on which an account had been carved in both Greek and Egyptian practically word for word. Now scholars who knew Greek could repeat the message in their own language. Next came letter-for-letter trackdown, and a Frenchman, Jean Francois Champollion, did most to establish that the hieroglyphics were sound syllables. Familiar names of the pharaohs and of a few places which had not been renamed by Greeks or Romans were the helpful clues, and soon a great deal besides cat history was eagerly read in the ancient writings.

Eventually Arab rule returned, and humble field workers could go on taking over the hillside tombs for their own housing; however, they resented the painted scenes of unknown gods and words that they could not read. So when strangers came along wanting to buy a few scenes to keep or sell, the field workers let

them hack out whatever chunks were easiest to dislodge. In time, vandals destroyed other scenes just for the sale of destruction, as vandals unfortunately still do almost everywhere.

Even in the twentieth century enterprising hucksters were finding or faking things to sell to tourists on city street corners. Museums were sometimes the purchasers, and some were eventually granted legal right to study, copy and photograph the tombs, murals and artifacts.

THE DATE 1950 B.C. MAKES THIS EARLY PROOF OF THE CAT'S LONG PRESENCE.

P. E. Newberry, *Beni Hasan*

WITH THE CAMERA'S EYE WE WALK INTO THE WORLD OF THE
PHARAOHS AND THEIR CATS.

Photograph by Egyptian Expedition, The Metropolitan Museum of Art.

In 1907 the Metropolitan Museum of Art in New York City began a thirty-year expedition to the Theban necropolis where some tombs were still untouched. Recording cat history was not their prime quest, but their collection and its summary booklet, *Egyptian Wall Paintings*, hold irrefutable proof that the m'yaow was a welcome member of Egyptian households, as well as a figure in myth and legend. There is no longer an excuse for writers to say that wildcats were "probably" tamed here.

No exact record of day, month or year of first taming can be proved, but no earlier taming as a general custom has been verified. As long as Egypt's own pharaohs ruled, they did not allow even one m'yaow to leave their boundaries.

These relics have been carefully studied by Egyptologists from the Metropolitan Museum of Art and other experts so that each can be dated to match the years of the pharaoh in whose reign they were completed. Other museums with Egyptian art in which cats appear follow this same system.

So far, the earliest evidence of tame cats comes in two paintings close to 2400 B.C. Tomb G5020 shows that palace chamberlain I-mery and his wife Ni-kau-Hathor have a daughter named M'yat. The other (Tomb CG95) had a cat among the family pets of court official Ti and wife Neferhetepes. Tomb 69 among many at Beni Hasan north of Thebes shows that tending to a cat and family pets was part of a house servant's daily chores in 1950 B.C.

A more satisfying trackdown on cat history trail comes with a photograph of Theban tomb 181 decorated in 1880 B.C. and seen some three thousand years later by Metropolitan archaeologists. Plaster is missing here and there leaving tantalizing blanks, but enough of original shapes and colors remain so that a little searching for familiar cat silhouette carries the eye to the picture's right-hand edge showing a cat serenely at ease under a lady's chair.

This was no once-in-a-lifetime pose for cats in ancient Egypt. In Egypt training a favorite female cat to sit under its lady's chair had become an established custom. They were there at

SPOILING A CAT WAS AS EASY FOUR THOUSAND YEARS AGO AS IT IS NOW.

The Metropolitan Museum of Art (30.4.114).

mealtime. Perhaps tied there at first, as is shown in earlier Tomb 130 of 1450 B.C., the cat learns what is expected and comes of its own accord. This custom came from superstitious belief that the female cat's skill in having so many healthy, well-behaved babies came as a gift of magic from Bastet the cat goddess, and would somehow be passed to the lady in this close companionship. What praise for the cat and lady both, when their hoped-for babies did appear!

Two murals, among many others, give unmistakable proof of how pampered and petted m'yaows had become. In 1275 B.C., sculptor Ipuy of the Craftsmen's Village (TT217) is pictured allowing a kitten to test its claws on the sleeve of a very handsome robe. His wife, Duammeres, has given the mother cat a silver collar plus silver rings for her nose and ear. Take a second look at the mother cat's coat as well as the dark, bespeckled pattern and at those large ears and you know it is a descendant of *Felis chaus*, the Jungle Cat. Mummies of cats at Bubastis also show this pattern. Wildcats that wear it are still seen in Egypt.

Even more doting tolerance for m'yaow exuberance was part of family life in the royal household of Amen-hotep III and his wife, Queen Tiye. A mural in the tomb of the queen's brother Anen (T120, 1380 B.C.) shows three lively pets—m'yaow, goose and monkey—romping through the throneroom, no doubt scattering all kinds of treasures in their haste to be first to claim victory under the queen's throne. Was the m'yaow first, then drawing the goose in to share, but with hissing scorn sending the monkey scooting away for cover? Missing plaster suggests a battle, but at least the cat's arm holds the goose gently. Restore those missing parts and it's surely just a game.

CATS AS COMPANIONS

The cat, if a female, might have been the adored companion of the couple's firstborn son. He called her Ta-myt (*Ta* implies importance) and when she died he had a special coffin (now in the Egyptian Museum at Cairo) carved for her. Domed lid and four sides are decorated with her pictures and symbols for prayers

IS THIS A THREE-WAY BRAWL OR A GAME OF TAG? COULD YOU TELL
IF ALL THAT PLASTER WEREN'T MISSING?

THE FALLING PLASTER LEFT JUST ENOUGH CLUES FOR THE AUTHOR
TO REPLACE MISSING FUR AND FEATHERS AND BE ASSURED ALL WAS
JUST A GAME.

Restored with permission of the
Metropolitan Museum of Art.

that the gods receive her kindly and grant that she no longer be
weary, but would shine forever in the night sky as a never-fad-
ing star.

Perhaps the prince would search for her star when he missed
her most, looking among those long-known to the priests for
their special link to the gods or goddesses. One especially was
dedicated in part to Bastet, the cat goddess. It reappeared each

Janice Lovoos

year after some absence just as the River Nile reached its flood-time of bounty to restore the fields and all growing things, and so begin the new year. In Greece it would be named Sirius, the dog who accompanied the hunter Orion, but for a heartbroken Egyptian prince who loved his cat and knew the legends of his own land, it would be the perfect place to seek a small twinkle of light, hope for a prayer to be granted.

Other m'yaows were also cherished as loved and loving companions in the centuries that followed. Egyptians still revered those with sun-bright fur as an other-self of the Sun god, the reason m'yaows must never be allowed to leave Egypt's boundaries.

However, as prosperity relied more and more on exporting wheat and barley, more and more value was placed on the cats' mousing skills. Now Greek and Phoenician sea-traders who came to buy grain were demanding a m'yaow to guard each cargo. They were refused, of course. Who dared anger the Sun god and disobey the pharaoh?

Somehow the Phoenicians and Greeks acquired m'yaows without bringing vengeance upon themselves. Between the years 610 and 595 B.C. the pharaoh accepted the Greek offer to provide him with Egypt's first navy, complete with elite crews and officers. Phoenicians helped design a canal linking the Nile to the tip of Suez Gulf and charted trade routes down to the Red Sea and beyond. Both needed their own quarters ashore, of course, so they moved in. Later, at sea again, they had m'yaows aboard.

How did that happen? Egyptians were too involved with internal rebellion and invaders to have time to question. Perhaps the pharaohs didn't hear about it till too late for action. After all, m'yaows were still plentiful throughout the land, still beloved and highly prized by all.

But now the trail that marks cat history leads from Egypt westward across the Mediterranean to the Atlantic and back again and the years when M-Y-W turned into C-A-T.

FROM M-Y-W TO C-A-T

As the sixth century B.C. began, the news that the Greeks were back from Egypt with six pairs of m'yaows spread from one Mediterranean port to another. When questioned, the Greeks admitted they'd soon have young mouse-catchers for sale, but did not call them m'yaows. Instead they discreetly used the name already given to whatever small furry predators they'd been trying to tame as mousers, with only small success.

The name *ailouros*, derived from *aiol* (ever-moving) and *ouros* (tail), fit the Egyptian newcomers even better than it did the weasels, stoats and stone martens already included in the tail-waver category. They were all clever at twitching the tip of a tail to misdirect the gaze of unwary prey, but none achieved the m'yaows' aristocratic grace or the variety of messages their wigwag signals conveyed only to those who understood. As fewer and fewer of the weasel clan were kept for mouse patrol, the name became more and more only for cats. In 460 B.C. the Greek traveler-historian Herodotus wrote of the ailouros he'd seen in Egypt, as if this were the only name to use.

The Phoenicians, who also came home with m'yaows, never talked about them. Like all the rest of the knowledge that brought their sea-trading success, it was nobody's business but their own. Once cats were offered for sale, however, word got around fast. Luckily, they had enough ships and crews to deliver at more than one port. For the past three centuries they had been establishing a chain of trading posts to the Mediterranean's western-most shores. Sicily first, with Carthage and Utica opposite on the African mainland, then Malta and Sardinia and on to Ibiza. Gadir

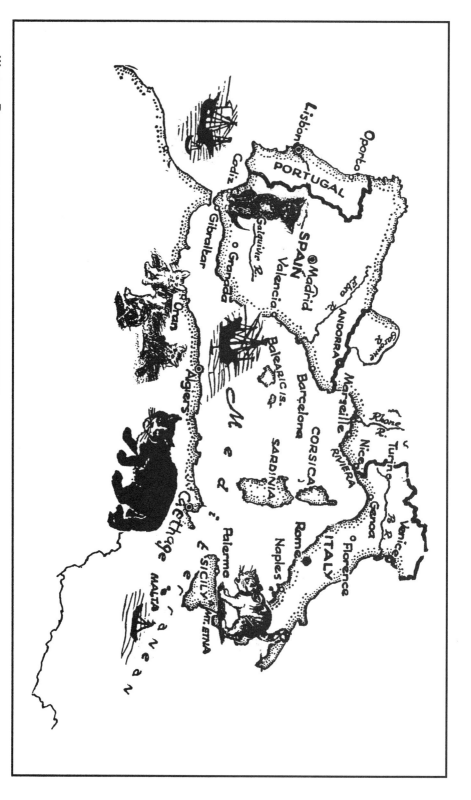

(Cádiz) and Tartessus, both Atlantic Ocean ports, were last. No one else had sailed so far. No one else would spread the good news of cats for pets so far and so fast.

Soon they would have some twenty-six posts along the shores of Carthage, Morocco, Algiers. Today's archaeologists who have puzzled over finding the ancient bones of the African Wildcat so far from home should have posted the reminder PHOENICIANS WERE HERE on their maps. Others have put it on maps elsewhere without the proof of dated artifacts that exist in the Mediterranean. The Sicilian historian Diodorus believed they had gone north all the way to Cornwall and Ireland for a valuable cargo of tin. Herodotus wrote that one crew had actually sailed down the Red Sea to the Indian Ocean and around Africa's cape and up Atlantic shores to Gibraltar's strait in a three-year wonder-trip. Others said they'd also gone east to India, perhaps for ivory, apes and peacocks like those the Bible reports were for Solomon.

How Do *You* Spell Cat?

Almost everything written in these years had to be credited to the Phoenicians, for they were first to put together a phonic alphabet. Each sign was the sound of a single consonant, not an entire word or syllable, with no pictures for a reminder. The idea was copied so fast by so many that the originators scarcely had a chance to take a bow. Later as they traded closer home— Syria, Cyprus, Rhodes, north to the Aegean and then east to the Greek colony at Byzantium on the Bosporus Strait—they may have learned a new word for the ailouros-m'yaow.

Just how the Byzantines themselves had learned this word isn't certain, but the opportunity was there in 514 B.C. when Persian armies came north on sweeping takeover marches from the Persian Gulf to the Black Sea and made the Greek colony their final conquest. The Byzantines would remain under Persian rule for thirty-six years and so had their chance to meet with traders from other Persian conquests farther south and learn new words and ways. Till then, the strait had been a barrier, but now Persian troops would have welcomed traders, and eager Byzantines could at least listen in on deals and dickering.

THE LANDS WHERE M'YAOWS BECAME CATS.

Vendors from Phrygia were nearby and would have come most often. They had settled there long before the Greeks tried an eastern colony, one of several bands of northern nomads with an ancient claim in the area. Now in Byzantium markets, they would display their wares: expertly woven carpets, handsome embroideries, tools for craftsmen, musical instruments and prized work in bronze and silver. Just as welcome were their news items, gossip and small talk.

Did they also bring pelts of wildcats and other animals? Or could watchers chuckle over the antics of a pet wildcat held on leash? Surely others besides the Greeks and Phoenicians took advantage of relaxed vigil at Egyptian ports or had managed to get pets from Nubia. Or had these southerners tamed pets themselves? African Wildcats, Jungle Cats and Indian Desert Cats were all in the area though never seen across the strait in Byzantium. Or did they see only carved cat figures or likenesses on tapestry?

"What animal is that?" Byzantines would have asked, pointing, letting raised eyebrows or a shoulder shrug speak for them if they lacked words the vendor would understand. The answers from Phrygians—or Armenians or any of the other people of northern descent—would sound much alike as they still do today. Usually each had two syllables, the initial consonant **G** or **K,** or perhaps a breathier **GH** or **KH** with **D** or **T** in the middle and an "uh" sound on the end.

Most of the many Phrygian writings are lost except for a few inscriptions on monuments, so their spelling can't be checked now. But the Armenian word has survived, and is usually written *gadu*. To Caucasus Mountain nomads it was *kat* or *kato*. Among Semitic tribes learning the word, Syrians heard *kato* but Aramaeans wrote *khatu*. Arabs chose *qit*, but their *q* is equal to *k*, so there's small difference. Byzantine Greeks used three spellings: *katta, gatto, khatta* (*kh* = *x—chi*). When the word reached Athens, scholars usually chose *katta*, and then somehow the meaning got as mixed as the spelling. Oddly, the error was made by Aristophanes, one of their most famous poet-playwrights, famed for keeping his listeners chuckling. His spelling matches our *gale* and no one seemed to doubt he meant the ailouros. No correction was ever made, but scholars ever since have been wondering what was so funny about hexing cats with this warning: If a *gale* crosses your path, it's bad luck. Furthermore, another famous dramatist, Theophrastus (also trying for a laugh from the audience), added this threat: If a *gale* crosses your path as you begin a journey, you'll never finish it!

Where did they get this idea? The only likely solution is that they didn't mean cats, but another species sharing the ailouros label. Think twice—or maybe only once—and you know the only possible choice. It's still confused with cats in English—the polecat, of course. *Mustela putoris* by Latin label; in Old English *poul*-cat from the root word for poultry. It's a European species and, like its American relatives the skunks, can soak pursuers with a most foul odor, so that an encounter would indeed send the traveler home in a hurry. As Rome took over from Greece as leader, these and other Greek classics were forgotten in Europe and so the disastrous impact of this bad-luck label didn't have full force till the Middle Ages. Then Greek was scholar's fare again. Oxford collegians turned *gale* into *galoot*—slang for anything despicable—and cats have been linked with evil and misfortune ever since.

Meanwhile, the Byzantine **G, K,** and **KH** had all three been ignored by the Romans in developing their own version of the alphabet that Greeks had copied from the Phoenicians, adding a few letters of their own. Carving letters into stone with a hammer in one hand and a chisel in the other was no longer the only way to create lasting records. Sharp stylus or brush took only one hand, and the smoothness of calfskin, sheepskin or goat hide invited the grace of curved letters instead of Greek straight lines. Among other changes, Roman scribes curved the straight angles of the Greek Γ (their *g*) and gave *c* the sounds of *K* or *S*. They moved Γ down to seventh place and curved it, too, adding a crossbar on the upturned tip. They kept *k* but seldom used it, letting their new *c* take its place. So for Romans, *katta* became *catus*—with the last syllable changing to show gender, plural or grammatical value according to their rule for all nouns.

PATIENCE PROVES A CAT A CAT.

This was the alphabet they brought with them as Caesar's legions swept north to England. There, sometime after A.D. 43, they began four centuries of teaching Roman ways and speech to any Britons who were willing to learn. Only those who became fluent in Latin could aspire to official positions, land ownership, a share in their own government and Roman luxuries. Romans had brought families and pets with them, and having a cat soon became a privilege Britons enjoyed all the more because their native wildcats could never be tamed.

A CAT BY ANY OTHER NAME

When the Romans were finally forced to leave—ordered back to help defend Rome from invasion—Britons happily kept their cats but rejected Latin endings as too much bother, and over the years *catus* changed to *catte* or *catt* and finally *cat* in everyday speech.

Britons also learned the Latin word *felis*, which Romans had coined for themselves before borrowing Greek *katta*. Whether it came from *felix* (which means happy, contented, lucky) or *furis* (rascal, thievish) has never been settled. However, Romans were truly fond of cats, and *furis* may have to be content with responsibility for *ferret*, the name for a lighter-colored polecat that could usually be trusted to withhold its spray power. (Its

American relative, the Black-footed Ferret, *Mustela nigripes*, is a different species.)

Most dictionaries trace *cat* to *catus* and *catus* to Greek *katta*, deeming that the end of reliable roots. However, ancient Greeks borrowed many words from Phrygians who were in Thrace before moving southeast into Asia Minor, and so tracing *katta* to *gadu* is a logical step. If *cat* did not come straight to English from nomad tongues, the word *catch* appears to have had an ancient link to *gadu* and *katta* and their kindred, which strengthens the opinion that *gadu* to *katta* to *catus* to *cat* is indeed the right derivation and that *catch* shares the same roots.

And what did *catch* mean? According to linguists, the original meaning is closest to "lie in wait for and seize."

Lie in wait for and seize! That is the perfect description of a cat's hunting technique. So it's reasonable to conclude that ancient hunters of these nomad tribes named wildcats for their watch-and-pounce patience just as others elsewhere named them for a defiant hiss and Egyptians chose m'yaow. After all, scientific classification to mark catlike from doglike also relies on the difference between wait-and-seize and race-and-chase even today.

Medieval Europeans allowed *catus*—especially in its feminine form of *catta*—to keep the "long tail, waving tail" meaning of ailouros, which we have dropped. In 1550 the English thought the long woolly-coated larva of certain moths looked like a hairy tail off on its own and so called it *catyrpillyr*—and a few similar spellings of *pilus*, Latin for hair. Oddly, most dictionaries still report "hairy cat" as the literal meaning of *caterpillar*. Puzzling, too, are the cats in Baruch 6:21 that fly over pagan idols with bats and swallows. Here the old meaning is wagtail, a bird still known by that name, which in Latin is *motacilla*, "little mover."

In Italy the word for cat is *gatto* and in Spain it is *gato*. Both formerly were confused with the "long tail" meaning, too. When Marco Polo first saw long-tailed monkeys in the Orient, he described them in his diary as *gatta paula*. To him, the two

READERS COULDN'T TELL FACT FROM FABRICATION.

words were adjectives meaning "long-tailed and small." When Columbus read his journal in preparation for his own voyages, he mistook the adjectives for the name of a species. So he looked for long-tailed monkeys when he reached the land he thought was Asia, the only continent opposite Europe then shown on any map. He saw them at last on his third and fourth voyages, confidently reporting them as *gatto paulo*, and described the larger howler monkeys as bearded like a man and with a long tail it could wrap around the snout of a wild hog like an iron fist—a truly magical weapon.

Back in Spain, folk said he was lying because no animal had a tail like that. They don't in the *Old* World, only in the Americas. But German author Konrad Gesner ordered an artist to draw one for his book, *Historia Animalium*, published in 1551, using his imagination. He did, and even added babies riding on the back of this creature. Readers used this as another excuse to charge Columbus with lying.

They may also have disbelieved him when he said there were no horses on the islands he found on the first voyage. He also said there were no cows, sheep, goats, mules, oranges, wheat, olives—and nothing like cats, of course. Good barnyard mousers. Couldn't manage without them. Spanish folk would have to bring some if they expected to make a colony and mine for gold.

So he made his list, all the while remembering that first he would have to sail back across the ocean. No one before him had ever sailed this course full out-and-home-again.

4
CATS AND CHRISTOPHER COLUMBUS

On March 15, 1493, shortly before noon, Christopher Columbus stepped ashore at the little river-port of Palos on Spain's southwest coast. In spite of a storm-plagued crossing, he had done more than just complete the first-ever there-and-back-again Atlantic voyage. He had also returned to the very port from which he had set sail seven months before. No one now could doubt his seamanship. He had earned his title: Admiral of the Ocean Sea.

Most of his crew were Palos men and they were ecstatic. So were the cheering, shouting, joyfully weeping townsfolk gathering in welcome. Suddenly their clamor changed to disbelieving gasps of wonder.

Coming now behind Columbus and his officers were ten completely alien figures, black-haired, brown-skinned and bedecked from topknot to ankles in waving feathers and dangling, gleaming gold that included neck chains, pendants, nose rings, ear rings, bracelets, anklets, and wide-linked belts. Each carried a huge basket cage that held bright-feathered birds with big, curved beaks.

The watchers each in turn nudged one another, gestured toward the birds and grinned. Parrots! And everybody knew the old saying: Any land with parrots in the trees has gold underground. No further proof needed. Columbus had found the Indies. The land of treasures.

Their eyes were drawn away from parrots and gold ornaments only by the growing stack of bales, bundles and baskets watched

41

NOW COLUMBUS WAS ADMIRAL OF THE OCEAN SEA.

over by stern-faced guards. More treasures, of course. Probably the best of everything set aside for the king and queen.

Isabella and Ferdinand, as it happened, had no chance to see this spectacular arrival. They were far to the north in their palace at Barcelona. So Columbus sent a messenger with the good news and began arranging for a whole train of carts and wagons and guards and servants to take him to Barcelona. News of his coming preceded him. He had to stop at every town and city along the way, even at country crossroads, in order to let people see the Indians and at least the parrots, if nothing else. Every day the crowds gathered from Palos to Seville, then to Córdoba and Valladolid, and finally, in mid-April, Barcelona.

So, well before Isabella and Ferdinand had even a peek at Columbus's treasures, half of Spain had heard the story and had gone gold crazy. When the monarchs did see what he had brought, Columbus knew he could have anything he asked to help him found a colony on his favorite of all the Caribbean islands he had explored.

La Española, Little Spain, was what he had written on his map to mark the makeshift fort for the thirty-nine men left behind there. (Later, books reporting the name would turn it to Latin as *Hispaniola* or *Insula Hyspana*, Spanish Island, but those labels were not Columbus's choice.) *Española*, he said now, describing its balmy, year-round springtime greenery. And he brought out that long list he'd been making of all the things he must take back with him.

Cats may have seemed last and least of all the things being loaded aboard the seventeen ships of his new fleet ready to sail from Cádiz harbor on September 25, 1493, but on the flagship with Columbus was his old friend from teenage years, Michele de Cuneo, who'd come along as "gentleman adventurer" and evidently knew the value of good mousers. When he wrote his travel letter, cats were there with horses and cattle and everything else to give Little Spain the essence of Spain itself.

The fleet moved south down the bulging African shoreline and then west to pass the last of the Canary Islands. Now only ocean lay ahead. On his first voyage, having no chart to follow, Columbus had kept on due west. But now he veered southwest, hoping to sight the unknown mainland the island natives had heard about and then described, marvelling at its size. Only islands came into view, seeming no different from those he already knew, and he finally turned northwest toward Española. He found it, somehow, amidst the Caribbean's maze. He had a remarkable talent for getting where he was going on uncharted waters. But one glimpse from the deck told him the makeshift fort had been ravaged. Once on shore, he found no sign of life among tumbled ruins. Eventually a few Indians appeared, unwilling to answer his questions. Finally one of their leaders came and told him the Spaniards had been killed as punishment for the way they had forced the Indian men into endless

panning for gold and taken the Indian women to serve them without reward, as if they were slaves.

To the Indians, their deaths were justice, not murder, and they expected Columbus to see it the same way. They remembered how he had always ordered his men to trade fairly for what they wanted. Now that he was back they expected him to take control and deal fairly as before, unaware that he couldn't control these men as he had his crews. Indian girls entertained with a dance, singing to the tinkling music of metal clips on waving fingers. None tried to stop him when he said he would settle farther eastward along Española's north shore. A harbor he remembered there seemed to be a good place to build a real town. The harbor was ample. A high cliff promised safe lookout for attack. In his mind he'd already named it La Isabela for the queen, and everyone fell to work as he directed. Just reminding them that they could not pan for gold until the work was reasonably underway was enough to keep them at it. The place for panning was Cibao, just a little farther south, forever prodding them to hurry.

THE CATS OF LA ISABELA

So the cats of La Isabela, the first descendants of the Egyptian m'yaow in the New World, welcomed in the New Year of 1494 in a proper town, well laid out, even if still incomplete. The admiral's house stood apart on the cliff. Beyond it would be the church and beyond that several small dwellings for officials, then a large storehouse of many uses. All would have walls made of huge blocks of tamped earth to be thickly coated inside and out with lime plaster. Roofs were likely made of thatch in the beginning, like the roofs of Indian huts. The important ones would be neatly finished in red tiles as soon as a kiln could be readied to make them.

The cats were probably placed on mouse patrol duty in the storehouse. The admiral might have kept one for similar service in his own house, but there's no proof he did so. Even Cuneo didn't mention whether Columbus liked cats, or if he would want a pet as well as a mouser. But at least Columbus didn't dislike them—as some people do with considerable violence—or

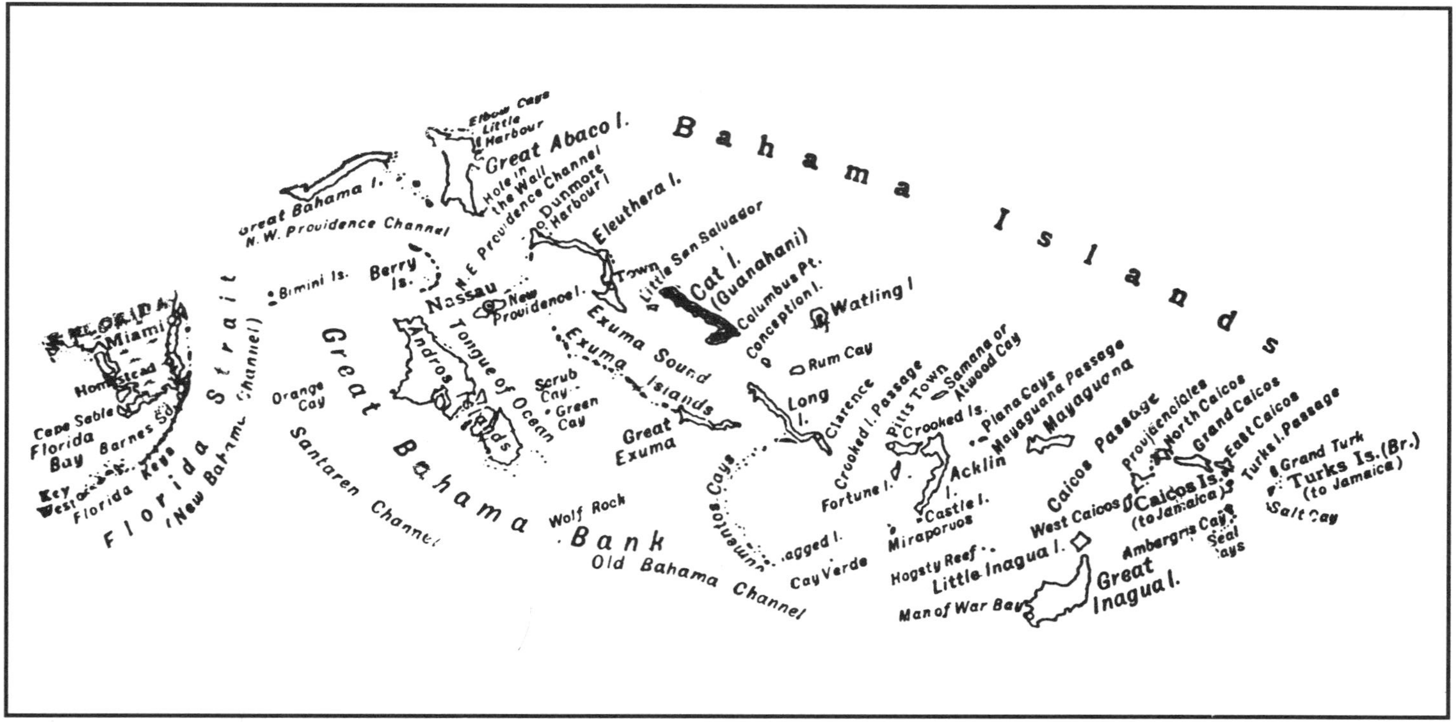

THE MAP SOLVES THE MYSTERY.

he'd have assigned them to another ship on the voyage out, not his own. And that's about as far as their story goes.

What happened to the cats of La Isabela is one more mystery in the chronicle of first-cat adventures. The town itself lasted only four years, a victim of too much sickness and rivalry and too little gold. Those who survived moved south to the New La Isabela, later part of Santo Domingo. Maybe cats and kittens did, too. Cuneo said they reproduced "in a superlative manner."

There seems small chance that any evidence of cats at the first La Isabela will be found, although restoration of the town began in 1992 as part of the Columbus Quincentennial and as a continuing tourist attraction. Much of its long-lost story is being revealed in the process, and if cats haven't been given a place as yet, they should be. Perhaps little life-size weather-proof statues of cats would be placed on windowsills or nestled in trees or offered as souvenirs for visitors.

Although the cats of La Isabela have nothing more to add at present, Columbus had one more link with cats and American history, even if he himself was unaware of it. The link is joined to a much larger unsolved riddle: the identity of the island on which he first landed on October 12, 1492.

CAT ISLAND

It was one of the outer Bahama Islands, that much is certain. But which one? He named it San Salvador, thus giving thanks to the Lord for safe voyage. The Taino Indians who lived there called it Guanahani, he noted in his journal. But there was no map of his anchorage, and he never returned to any of the first few little islands of his October landings. They were all too small to serve as a colony or trading post with the Asian mainland he always hoped to find. He gave some brief description of each, so general that nine different islands feel they can claim to be Guanahani. One among them is the present Cat Island, so named by the first British colonists who settled there.

Whoever named it must have known the reason, but it wasn't written down anywhere for later proof. And somehow the belief grew that this was Columbus's first landing isle and he had left the ship's cat there as proof. In 1806, when Noah Webster published the first edition of the famous dictionary, Columbus's first landing on Cat Island was included among his "remarkable events" but nothing was said of the gift of a cat being the reason for the name.

Other islands now seem to have prior claim, but Bahama Tourist Information Bureau officials continue to be badgered about namesake cats. This island, they reply, has no record of early cats or any unusual number of cats. Nobody seems to remember that plain English *c-a-t* came to mean several other things besides *Felis catus.* Webster, in 1806, lists cat ships, cat whips and cat fish. Later editions include a particular item of ship gear known as cat hook or just cat. If they also had a sketch of this "cat" beside a sketch of Cat Island, the likeness in bent-tip shape might have solved the riddle of Cat Island naming long ago.

CATS IN THE SPANISH COLONIES

There's less mystery and considerably stronger proof for other tales of cats in Spain's American colonies. Gonzalo Fernández de Oviedo, first official historian of the Indies, mentioned in his account of 1526 that many, many cats were taken to the colonies because none could be found wild or as tame native pets. Antonio de Herrera and Francisco López Gómara, both noted historians, agreed that cats were brought in large numbers. Gómara even thought they seemed happier in the New World than at home—did less yowling and had more kittens. In Peru, historian Garcilaso de la Vega told how a Spanish cat amused the Inca ruler Atahualpa, so soon to be murdered.

Veteran seafarers—among them the English freebooter Lionel Wafer—advised novice travelers to bring along a cat for trade with Indians. Might well be worth a bit of gold. Missionaries wrote of how cats attracted possible Indian converts, always delighted to stroke their fur or hear them hiss as fiercely as their big, wild cousins.

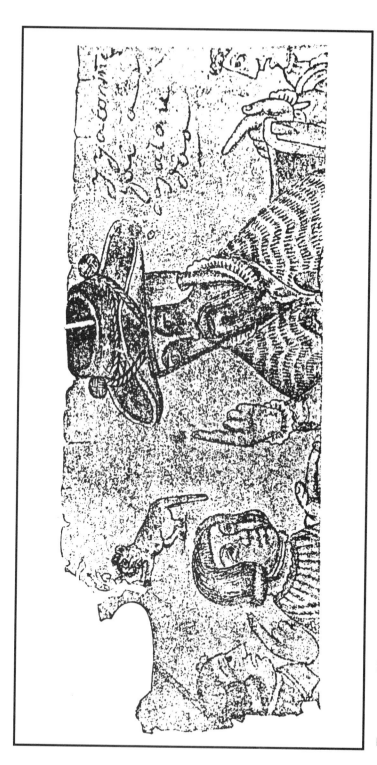

THIS SMUG MEXICAN PUSS SKETCHED IN *1541* BY A MIXTEC VILLAGE ARTIST MAY BE THE OLDEST PICTURED BY A NATIVE AMERICAN ANYWHERE IN THE AMERICAS.

Academia de Bellas Artes, Puebla, Mexico.

In Mexico, Indians of the Mixtec tribe saw their first cat in 1541 and were enchanted. It was probably the first cat ever to appear in the little village of Yanhuitlan, just a patch in the road—except for its church—between the larger towns of Puebla and Oaxaca. Even a bishop once came to visit that church. And since the bishop brought his cat, their arrival was an event. The cat, as it turned out, was an extrovert who liked attention, liked to poke its nose and paws into all sorts of places, liked to have an admiring audience.

One of the admirers there in Yanhuitlan was an artist. And when someone in authority—perhaps the mayor, perhaps the bishop—suggested a folio of pictures portraying village life under the Spaniards as a gift for the viceroy, the artist agreed. Of course he included the bishop in one scene—and the cat. It's there on an overhead perch, paws outstretched to investigate something the torn page doesn't reveal. The look on the cat's face suggests it was well aware this was a no-no. Did those paws get a firm hold before the command to stop came? That's another question never answered.

Also untold is the full story of how that picture, along with others by the same artist, turned up 350 years later in the Academy of Fine Arts at Puebla. But there it was, and the museum director sent it along to Madrid for display at the Columbus Quadricentennial in 1892.

Cats and Columbus and the first mingling of New World and Old on written records belong together no matter how the true story is told.

FIRST CATS FOR NORTH AMERICA

Any accounting of the first house cats as pets north of Mexico is bound to have could-be and might-be loopholes. The first Europeans to settle in this part of the Americas *could* have had a descendant of Egyptian m'yaows with them. They *might* have brought a mated pair and raised the first American-born kittens. But there's no proof they did. No written record, no skeletal remains, not even hand-me-down legends.

Vikings were the first European settlers, making a home in Labrador around the year A.D. 1000. They kept no journals, drew no maps, and eventually sailed home again with stories to tell that apparently said nothing of cats. For the next five hundred years many a tale was told of boats blown by Atlantic storm winds beyond familiar shores and of strange lands looming to westward. Crews that did not return may have found some North American port and stayed there. Fishermen did learn the way to the Grand Banks off Newfoundland, and returned to fish again, but not to settle with family and pets.

England began exploring the coastline by ship in 1497, France in 1534, but Spain made the first settlements. In 1526 a town of six hundred Spaniards was on the mainland across from today's Hilton Head Island but gone within the year. In 1559 their settlement at Pensacola, Florida, lasted two years. Twice, both in 1526 and in 1570, they landed near today's James River but were ousted by Algonkin Indians.

French Huguenots settled in 1562 on Parris Island, just across Port Royal harbor from Hilton Head, but were starved out by 1564. They refitted and tried again farther south along the

Portus Regalis, siue F S. Helena.

Prom. lupi.

St. John's River only to be wiped out by Spanish soldiers. In 1565, Spain reinforced its claim with the first European settlement in North America that still survives. San Agustin they called it, now St. Augustine, Florida. If any cats were there before 1609, the local historical society has yet to present proof.

THE FIRST ENGLISH SETTLEMENT

The first English settlement came in 1585, a little farther north at Roanoke in what is now North Carolina. Then it was part of the vast area claimed by England as the Virginia Colony. It seemed to thrive, but a supply ship docking in 1587 found it deserted. Even now, after much searching, no trace of the settlers has been found. English folk did not gather courage for another venture till 1607.

Three ships with 144 hopeful colonists aboard landed May 13, and 150 more followed on January 2, 1608. Among those serving in turn as president was John Smith, the first to publish their story. The site selected by their sponsors was farther north than Roanoke. Jamestown was on the James River, both named for their king. Here in the summer of 1609 rats were noteworthy, but apparently cats were not. Rats had been arriving on every ship. Rats and mice both were all ravenously hungry and unbelievably prolific in producing young. Till now they had been raiding with caution; this summer they dared invade the town's storehouses, not just a few but thousands, John Smith would declare in his next report. He added that the mice and rats were eating all they could hold, so befouling the storehouses with their droppings that he knew not how to keep what little they left.

Their grain had been limited to oatmeal and rice, since wheat doesn't travel well. Two friendly Indians taught them to plant corn, and others from the nearby village were willing to trade game for English tools and trinkets. With nothing more to trade, the colonists were on their own and far from expert. Some who went fishing couldn't throw the net right. Those hunting for nuts found only acorns. Sturgeon, it turned out, was so plentiful everyone grew sick of eating it—even the dogs, Smith said, and the fact that he didn't mention cats supports the general belief that none had arrived, even with later colonists. In 1978 biographer Noel B. Gerson wrote of seeing a memo among Smith's papers of his plan to lease cats from the next ship to drop anchor. So cats became a trade item. No supply ship came that summer. They ate the last of their livestock. Few escaped wracking fevers. The Starving Time, they called it, and Jamestown's population dropped from nearly five hundred to sixty.

In August two battered ships that had sailed from England with others—including the supply ship—limped into port. They'd been caught in a hurricane, each vessel scattered to fight the storm alone. They saw at least one sink with all aboard but they'd seen nothing of the *Sea Venture*, which was carrying all the supplies and the new governor for Jamestown and other notables. Now these luckier ships brought new colonists and a strict command from London for Captain John Smith to return at once.

Smith had no choice but to go. He sailed October 4, 1609, presumably taking with him the town's desperate plea for cats. The other ship stayed.

In Jamestown the new settlers felt free to do as they pleased. The agreement they'd signed seemed void after they had survived and the officials hadn't and staying in Jamestown meant working for food like a common laborer. Off they went to hunt for gold and live on woodland fruits and nuts and wild turkey and venison until the next ship came and they could go back to London like nabobs. Not one heeded the warning that the Indians had kept hunting rights beyond the area they had granted to the colonists. It was recorded that the Indians were ready to kill trespassers or take them hostage.

No one knew that the *Sea Venture* was jammed in the rocks on an island some Spaniards had discovered in 1515. They named the island Bermuda after their captain, Juan de Bermudez. They'd left some hogs for possible future castaways, as was custom, and survivors found plenty of tasty fruits and herbs as well. Hope and health restored, both crew and

HISTORIES OF JAMESTOWN, BERMUDA AND NEW ENGLAND CAME
FROM HIS BUSY PEN.

passengers set to building two smaller vessels from the ship's planks and fittings.

The rocks that held the *Sea Venture* in firm grip had protected it from tide and winds. Almost everything was in good shape. Still, building anew wasn't easy and a full eleven months passed before they were ready to sail for Jamestown. Two men decided to stay on Bermuda. The rest, undaunted settlers, the colony's new governor, Baron De la Warr, and their staff, including one Ralph Hamor, set out for Jamestown on June 12, 1610.

By this time, colonists old and new at Jamestown were desperate. Fearing themselves forgotten, they persuaded the remaining ship's captain to take them back to London. They had scarcely left harbor when they sighted the two ships with hurricane survivors. Those aboard saw them also and elatedly flagged them down for reunion. Soon De la Warr convinced the colonists to return and try again, serving them hearty meals of food he had aboard, and assuring plenty more was not far away. Their stomachs convinced, if minds were not quite sure, they once more settled in at Jamestown. One ship hastened back to Bermuda for the promised food and the other went back to England with full report of hurricane power—a story so dramatic that Shakespeare promptly used the scene for his next play, *The Tempest.*

At Jamestown, De la Warr became ill and asked George Percy, who had been there from the beginning and was a leader in the survival, to take charge. Along with his duties, Percy began making notes for the account of Jamestown hardships he meant to publish as soon as he got back to London. Two supply ships from the sponsors would arrive in 1611, one in May, the other in August.

There's a chance that cats were aboard, for Smith would say they brought "all that could be needful," and that *surely* included cats. Two more ships came in 1612. If either did have cats, no written record of it seems to have been found and reported.

JAMESTOWN IN 1622
VIRGINIA

[Enlarged from a cut in the *Scheeps-Togt van Anthony Chester Na Virginia, gedaan in het jaar 1620.* Printed at Leyden by Peter Vander, 1707. A pamphlet, 12mo.]

RESEARCHERS ARE STILL HOPING TO FIND THE REMAINS OF THIS HISTORIC SETTLEMENT THAT MAY HAVE BEEN WASHED OUT TO SEA BY STORMS.

Jamestown, however, is still the candidate for first settlement to have cats. George Percy declared in his memoirs, *Trewe Relacyons*, that he was among the hungry who ate them. "Having set upon horses and other beasts as long as they lasted, we were glad to make shift with such vermin as dogs, cats, rats and mice." What a fate for the first cats in what is now the United States of America!

Could starvation-stew really have been the sad end of the first cats at home in what is now the United States? Perhaps not. Percy certainly knew what he had eaten, or saw others eating, but his London publishers did not. Could they have added dogs and cats for shock value and bigger sales? Whatever the facts, the next known record of cats north of Mexico would also be at Jamestown.

This time there's no doubt. Ralph Hamor, who had come with De la Warr, was chosen as clerk of the town council. By 1614 he was ready to go home and was slated for return to London, but first he had to persuade Chief Powhatan to release a trespasser he still held captive and resume trade for furs the settlers could ship to England. This was the right time to ask, Hamor thought. The chief's daughter, Pocahontas, who had been a friend to John Smith, was living at Jamestown now and was the bride of John Rolfe, who had started the colony in the profitable business of growing tobacco, and Powhatan would frequently send his men to town for news of his daughter even if he wouldn't come visit her. Hamor sent word asking what was wanted for Will Parker's release and received this list written in Parker's hand:

> *10 pieces of copper, a shaving knife, an iron frow to cleave boards, a grinding stone not so bigge but 4 or 5 men could carry it, which would be bigge enough for his use, two bone combs such as Captain Newport had given him (the wooden ones his own men can make) 100 fish hooks or if he could spare it a fishing seine and a dogge and a cat.*

GRAY TABBIES AND GINGER TOMS ARE PHRASES OFTEN FOUND IN OLD DIARIES—ALONG WITH A WRY ADMISSION THAT SUPPOSED TOMS WERE SOMETIMES TABBIES.

Joyce Patelunas

A cat? Hamor must have thought. Surely rats hadn't gone that far inland or the chief would have demanded far more. Or perhaps Hamor guessed that spies the old chief had sent to report on Pocahontas had seen her playing with a cat and now wanted one for himself. But who in Jamestown would give up a family pet and faithful rat-catcher?

Somehow Hamor found a cat. His story of Jamestown days published in London in 1615 as "True discourse of the state of Virginia" adds only that he himself took the chief all he'd asked on May 15, 1614, and then returned with Will Parker and pelts as promised.

What color was this cat sharing the first diplomatic exchange between British colonists and North American Indians that involved a feline? Hamor did not say. Nor did he report whether cat and the chief became friends. Perhaps Hamor, safely back in London, would always wonder how the two got along.

The rest of us wonder, too. Probably it was a tabby—the most common pattern then as now—but gray tabby, brown or ginger-and-cinnamon? We do have a clue to the cat's Jamestown home, through watercolors by Richard Schlect in *National Geographic* (June 1979). These depict a nearby settlement begun in 1622 and only recently discovered after long burial by flood debris, as were the Jamestown ruins. Both had streets and houses encircled by a solid plank fence seven feet high. Each house had sheds for stock, a small garden and a lower fence. There's even a white cat in one sketch (*National Geographic*, page 764), and cat bones may be found in Jamestown ruins if they're discovered, too, one day.

Later, in the mid-1620s, when Captain John Smith was preparing his "Generall Historie" of England's American colonies, he included Ralph Hamor's trade for Will Parker, but didn't mention combs, cats or dogs. Instead he named the tools and ended with "fish hookes and such toies." He couldn't consider cats mere playthings, however, when he came to the story of Bermuda. Summer Isles was his name for the new colony there, originally Sommers' Isles, honoring the first governor. The change could have been mere misspelling or a clever way of encouraging settlers with a reminder of its balmy climate. Colonists did come, apparently without cats, and by 1615 Bermuda was besieged by rats.

By 1617 rats had taken over the main island and all of its surrounding coral islets. Smith judged them a plague sent by God to punish human sinners and credited God for their final extermination in spite of admitting that cats had been sent for, and did arrive, in some numbers. "Wilde and tame," he said,

FEW CATS WERE LOLLING ON SILKEN CUSHIONS IN THE NEW AMERICAN COLONIES. THEY PAID THEIR WAY WITH HARD WORK.

A CAT AND A BROOM MADE THE KITCHEN HOME, EVEN WHEN ANOTHER HOME WAS HALF A WORLD AWAY.

meaning some were former pets but mostly street cats as fierce as their wild ancestors.

The colonists abetted the cats with traps set nightly and trained ratting dogs and setting fire to rat-nesting colonies.

Finally rats were so few that any cat could police its own home territory. Each now found a family where it was welcome and moved in to stay. Smith gave them no applause, only complained that they hadn't ousted the rats sooner. History is indebted to Smith for his records, but cats don't even owe him a tail swish.

Some who write of first cats in the United States begin with Pilgrims aboard the *Mayflower*, forgetting that 1620 is really a late date in the nation's history than was Jamestown. Even then they have little satisfaction, for sources don't agree. One text may say that family pets were aboard the ship, mostly cats, dogs and birds. The next will claim that officials at the memorial Plymouth (Plimoth) Plantation say there is no documentary proof cats were aboard the *Mayflower* or if they arrived later.

Obviously cats did arrive. Travel-writer John Josselyn found them about as common here as in England by 1637. Three years earlier, another traveler named William Wood had seen them in Massachusetts winning full appreciation for their skill at chasing rats, mice, squirrels and birds from the just-planted little hills of corn kernels. Word soon spread that keeping a cat on duty during planting and three weeks thereafter was the only sure way not to lose half the crop before it could sprout. No need for scarecrows when you had a cat.

All in all, the facts available fully justify naming Jamestown in Virginia Colony when credit for the first cats in the forty-eight contiguous states is assigned. As for its being first in North America, no word of dispute will probably come from Alaska or even Hawaii, if it claims continental boundaries as well as statehood. Mexico accepts a Central America label.

Canada, however, will probably call for proof. Any well-read historian can point out that their St. Lawrence River country was claimed by France more than seventy years before English ships sailed for Jamestown. France had cats before England, since Gauls were conquered ahead of Britons on Julius Caesar's conquest march. So . . . ?

So exploratory vessels on Canada's coast do not prove cats went ashore or were even aboard. The land beyond the St. Lawrence River had been claimed for France in 1534 by Jacques Cartier. The French continued to come and go, but made no permanent settlement. Finally, on July 3, 1608, explorer Samuel de Champlain set up a trading post at the mouth of the St. Lawrence. *Kay-bek* was the local Micmac tribal name for the site and Champlain was content to borrow it. Spelling it, of course, was his own responsibility since the tribes had no written symbols. *Québec* was his choice, and so it remains. Champlain ordered his crew to build a three-story house to hold offices, workrooms and living quarters for all, and let the

Indians know he was ready to trade. The Indians were ready, too. They'd already had a taste of the remarkable wares the French could offer.

Back in France the various religious orders were eager to convert Québec tribes. Missionary priests and friars of the Récollet Order began arriving in 1615 and Jesuits were there by 1624. Both followed the same pattern, meeting tribal chiefs at the trading post and asking for an invitation to visit some inland village with their story. One who did so with considerable success was Père Gabriel Sagard, but he certainly got off to a bad start.

He must have heard of Jamestown's need for cats. Perhaps he also read Hamor's book and learned that Chief Powhatan had asked for a cat of his own. Hoping that the gift of a cat would be the sure way to win Indian acceptance, he decided two cats would be even better and arrived with a handsome pair, male and female. Surprisingly, the Huron chief who had consented to talk with him about a visit now eyed the cats with what seemed resentment. Sagard asked his interpreter to explain again how useful they would be. How both this pair and their descendents would chase away the crows and mice and rats—especially the rats—that had been stealing the village corn. With cats on guard there would be no more stealing.

The chief accepted the caged cats, but his face showed only cold courtesy. Sagard, thoroughly puzzled, asked the interpreter to explain again, adding that other chiefs elsewhere had been delighted with animals like these. And now the chief let his resentment show clearly. He was insulted—not pleased—to have foreigners think their caged animals could do more than the wild creatures of his own woods. Belatedly, Sagard realized that rats from French ships were not yet a menace beyond control here. Nevertheless, the gift had been offered and accepted and it was too late to restore goodwill, even with the interpreter's help. As soon as the expected politeness allowed, he went on to another village. Presently he learned that the scorned cats had died in their cage without producing any kittens.

Later, as more and more French families arrived—and with them the usual rats—cats were more than welcome in Québec. But the first ones never had a chance.

A CAT BY ANY OTHER NAME

Back in Europe, more attention was being paid to the need for each kind of animal or plant to have one universal, official name that everyone could recognize. Many of them then had so many different names even in the same language, that no one could keep them all in mind. Migrant species and others common in more than one country had different names in each language. The same folk name, even the same museum label, might be used for different species in different areas.

Some way to definitely designate each plant or animal was needed. Scholars, museum directors, college professors and medical men concerned with proper identification for herbs and animal organs used in their doctoring talked it over again and again. On one point they all agreed. The official name had to be in Latin, the one language every educated person in western Europe and the Americas understood. So in this case using Latin wasn't just being scholarly or showing off. It was necessary.

6

THE CASE OF THE NECESSARY LATIN

Almost all naturalists in mid-eighteenth-century Europe agreed on Latin names for universal use. In 1758, Karl Linnaeus of Sweden, a medical doctor as well as a professor of botany at Uppsala University, declared himself the one for action. Recently the names have been getting longer and longer—difficult to remember even for experts. Also, the same name was given to different species. He discarded all the wordy labels he'd concocted in his long career and published a new list with each label just two words. Two were enough, he informed all who would listen, if the *first* word named the group and the *second* gave the plant or animal some individual meaning. The Latin word for such a group would be *genus* and the unique individual type would be a *species*. Both were Latin words meaning "kind" or "sort." Now each had its own meaning.

Linnaeus asked all other naturalists to discard their old lists and use his. Any species not on his list could be named by whoever was first to get a genus and species in print with proper description. Printed date of publication settled priority. Brevity, priority, uniformity were the Linnean keys to permanent names for worldwide use. Linnaeus's 1758 list was brought out as the beginning of official names for nature's species.

A name for the house cat was on that famous list of 1758, making it first of the first if any argument came up later. *Felis catus* was the choice of both Linnaeus and the earlier British classifier John Ray to give future pets a one-name-fits-all label on scientific records. Linnaeus's description of a patchy coat color pattern not seen on wildcats proved beyond a doubt that he had only pets in mind. This point would one day deny the insistent claim of

THE REST OF THE WORLD TOOK A LONG TIME TO ADMIT THAT LINNAEUS WAS RIGHT ABOUT BRIEF SCIENTIFIC LABELS ACCEPTED WORLDWIDE.

certain British advocates that Linnaeus had meant the label for the European Wildcat, not enrolled as *Felis silvestris* until 1777. Undoubtedly, every wild species was in existence before the m'yaow, but for science, Linnaeus's 1758 is the Year One.

SWIRLS INSTEAD OF FAMILIAR TABBY STRIPING SEEMED SO WRONG THAT IT WAS CALLED BLOTCHED—ANOTHER WORD FOR BLEMISH.

The system Linnaeus devised, however, has undergone many changes. One of the first and most important was creating a label for species that shared certain broad likenesses in spite of major differences. Eventually the accepted title was *family*. For those of genus *Felis* and their kin, the Latin label is *Felidae*, with *id* standing for *idem* (similar, like) and *ae* a Latin plural. The English translation is "catlike ones." It is not a parent-child-uncle-cousin family of cats, but rather a group of catlike species.

If Linnaeus had been alive at the time this was approved, he would surely have agreed with the idea. But he might have suggested that "family," with its well-established meaning of close and current kinship, might lead to misunderstandings. For the

Felidae that is certainly true. People persist in calling lions, tigers and the other large species "big cats."

Perhaps it began in 1837 when *Routledge's Young Gentlemen's Magazine* described a circus tiger, adding a wish that one could pet that "pussy . . . such a blood-thirsty brute." At least it's true that this misguided attempt at humor has until recently been used only for cats (felids). *Cat* entering English from Roman *catus* was a name for tame cats only. Wolves, foxes, coyotes and jackals of the family Canidae aren't generally called dogs. Nor are zebras and asses called horses, yet the scientific family bond is the same.

Linnaeus did indeed list all catlike species in genus Felis, but he didn't have today's more precise to guide him. Not even the lynx and a few others of cat size are in other genera, as are all of the large felids except *felis concolor*—known as *puma* to Incas, *cougar* to Brazil's Tupi tribes and *mixtli* to the Aztecs. To early English-speaking Americans it was a mountain lion, catamount, panther and other folk labels still in confusing use.

PROOF OF IDENTITY

In Oregon, a newspaper headline "Ancient Cat Bones Found Here" had some readers believing direct ancestors of their pets larger than tigers lived in prehistoric Oregon. And a Florida newspaper presented readers with this puzzler: "Cats were here long before Columbus. Scientists say there's statuary evidence that small cats were domesticated here in Florida before Columbus set sail."

The "statuary evidence" offered as proof of this claim turned out to be a six-inch figure carved from an ancient piece of dark-colored, close-grained wood. It was found in May 1895 on Key Marco, an island off Florida's southern Gulf Coast, where it had been lying buried in mud and muck with other tribal artifacts for five hundred years or more.

You'll find it at the Smithsonian now. There it sits in a serene upright pose, tongue lolling for tidy lip-licking after a tasty meal. Any passing two-year-olds will name it for you with "Kitty cat!"

or whatever name they call the tiger from the box of animal crackers.

Smithsonian experts, of course, use *Felis concolor*, Latin for this American species with such a troublesome collection of names. Obviously, whatever source the Oregon reporter consulted did refer to it as a *cat*.

One book guilty of just such error is *Centuries of Cats* (Silvermine Publishers, 1971). A "cat effigy" in pre-Columbian Florida is one of their references to supposed pet cat ancestors seen on ancient pottery, stonework, metalwork and weaving. They are labeled "cats"—no use of "big" or other modifiers. The entire text makes it plain that only housecat ancestors are involved. So neither authors nor reporter understood that all cats are felids, but not all felids are cats.

In all families, each species is unique yet all are alike in certain ways. Felids share these likenesses:

1. Roundish head and jawline—some less rounded than others but none with the long snout of doglike Canidae species.

2. Claws that extend or retract quickly, not the fixed claws of Canids. (Cheetahs' claws retract only part way.)

3. Hunting technique—a patient wait-and-seize, or a crouch-and-creep advance, not the usual running chase of many canids. Among felids, only a cheetah goes full speed, but a jaguarundi is a fair sprinter.

Today's housecats inherit these traits from their wild ancestors. Watch one on a mouse hunt, even a catnip mouse, and you see the same defining features and hunting techniques of wild cat species. The Latin label of the housecat was chosen to name the entire family, only because Europeans who coined the label knew it best. "Like a cat" gave far better clue for comparison than naming lion or tiger most people saw only in zoo lethargy or not at all. Today the camera has made these largest felids familiar, but their ways were little known in Europe or the

Cats were here long before Columbus. Scientists say there's statuary evidence that small cats were domesticated here in Florida before Columbus sighted land in the Bahamas.

Americas when "catlike" became the official family recognition tag. Basic likeness is still there for mutant cats with long hair instead of short, or slanted eyes instead of round. So they also earn scientific rank under the *Felis catus* label. Each small difference gives identity as a separate breed, but not as a distinct species or subspecies. Except for domestic cats, dogs and horses, species labels are used only for wild animals whose differences have been determined by nature and established without human interference in choice of mates. Occasional new species are still being discovered.

THE "EVIDENCE" WAS A SIX-INCH CARVING WITH A COUGAR HEAD AND VAGUELY HUMANIZED BODY.

Three breeds of longhaired cats were seen in western Asia for the first time and eventually reported by European travelers with wondering admiration, each at a different time. The first two are still the best known: Angoras and Persians. Although they've been known even in the United States for over a century, for many the big question here and in Europe is still *How do you tell them apart?*

7

ENTER THE LONGHAIRED BEAUTIES

Distinguishing longhaired cats as *Angora* or *Persian* has become so confused that the two words must be untangled before either has the right meaning. Both names are equally misused, but *Angora*—an ancient Phrygian city some two hundred miles south of Byzantium—was first on cat history records.

PERSIAN AND ANGORA—WHICH IS WHICH?

Neither longhaired cats nor the word *Angora* were on record in the sixth century B.C. when invading Persians took over the territory and Byzantine Greeks learned the word that became the English word *cat*. Nor were longhairs on known records there in 334 B.C. when Greeks ousted Persians and Arabs, or in 133 B.C. when Romans took full command.

Sometime in those years the name was written *Enguri*, but Romans quickly changed it to *Ancyra*, replacing the *g* with their *c* as they often did. No word yet of longhaired cats. But the name Ancyra would be on so many maps and written records that there can be no doubt of its site or importance.

The city had been important in Phrygian times, too. It had been a thriving trade center for three hundred years or more before the Persian conquest. It was well fortified and a meeting place for much-traveled roads that the Persians would improve and lengthen as their own Royal Road north. Ruins prove it was built on a rocky hilltop overlooking a deep gorge and a river at some time named Enguri-Su. *Su* goes with river names, so "city-by-the-gorge" and "river-in-the-gorge" seem reasonable translations. It probably derives from ancient Sumerian *Enke*, god of the Abyss.

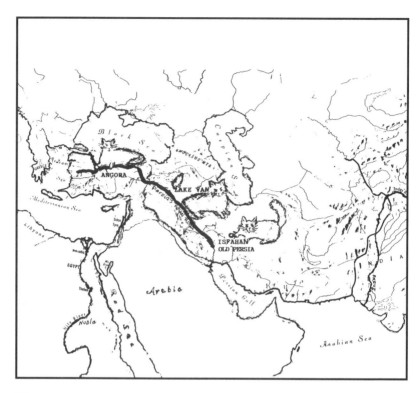

THE LAND OF THE FIRST LONGHAIRS—LIKE THE LAND OF OZ—IS FOUND BY FOLLOWING A FAMOUS ROAD.

Under Roman rule as Ancyra it became the capital of a district renamed Galatia because an adventurous band of Gauls had settled there in the third century B.C. By A.D.192 the people at Ancyra had become Christians and built a church. Most of the people were still Christians in 1067 when an army of Seljuk Turks laid siege and took over the city.

In 1360 a band of Celtic Crusaders—mostly French—arrived at Byzantium on their way to Jerusalem by land instead of sea. Now they learned they could fight the Turks and rescue Christians much nearer than Jerusalem, and on they went to Ancyra, pledged to victory. They kept that pledge and held off Turkish raids for a good eighteen years, and—almost beyond doubt—became the first Europeans to see cats with beautiful long silken fur and feathery tails that waved as proudly as the plumes on a knight's helmet.

Before Turkish raiders finally won, did any Crusaders escape to take news of those cats back to France? Or had any managed to send back word of their first victory—and the cats? Somehow they did, though copies of their messages seem to have disappeared and only rumors and vague echoes told of the new word *Angora*—their spelling of the city's name as they heard it—that would become the name for these longhaired cats.

Modern Turks changed it again, making it Ankara, and their national capital, with *Ank* the accented syllable. Rewrite the older names to match that division and ENG-uri, ANC-yra and ANG-ora sound enough alike to share the "by-the-gorge" meaning with Ankara. Spelling a Turkish word the Turkish way is courteous and reasonable, but Angora has been too well established in American and European usage to change easily. It has become the synonym for longhaired and used to describe any fur or synthetic yarn of the same soft silken touch. But where cats are concerned it needs to be clearly separated from Persian. Each has its own story.

The word *Persia* was coined by the Greeks as they misspelled *Parsa*, the name of an ancient northern tribe that had settled along the east bank of what is now the Persian Gulf. In 550 B.C. this tribe took over the Medes and other nearby settlements, welding them into a kingdom and leading them on those famous conquests north and west along old trade routes that soon would be named the Persian Royal Road. In time, stronger Greek armies would drive them back down that road to their old Parsa territory.

Perhaps shorthaired cats, descendants of the m'yaow, came with them to be the first feline pets in Persia. Or perhaps they found pet cats already there, either obtained from passing caravans from the west or the offspring of local wildcats—or from the mating of m'yaows and local wildcats. African Wildcats didn't roam this far on their own, but Jungle Cats and Indian Desert Cats did. Native species were the reddish-furred Sand Cat, *F. margarita* (also in Egypt) and Pallas's Cat, *F. manul*, more at home farther north and east. So far, no realiable account has been found to verify the first appearance of longhaired cats with the chubby body, round face and short legs that help distinguish Persian from Angora. However, it is certain both were seen before a third longhaired breed appeared near Lake Van in territory that had been both Persian and Armenian. However, Van cats, like the Angora, carry a name that identifies their place of origin with an exactness "Persian" denies.

Help came in 1871 from a British naturalist, William T. Blanford, who recorded his opinion that longhairs had first been seen in Isfahan, Persia's old capital. He also firmly stated that this Persian was distinctly different from both Angora and Van, and made it part of an official government report on his surveys of India's boundaries. His reputation from other surveys, and being quoted in *Encyclopaedia Britannica*, gave it considerable weight, even if most people back in England went right on confusing Angora and Persian.

Isfahan, then, is a good place to start in a search for early evidence of Persian cat presence. It was always a city of importance, a capital of the province when a change in political power gave another city the national rank. It was a city of elegance, luxury and charm with lavishly adorned palaces and pavilions and lush gardens to testify to wealthy owners with a love for all things beautiful—including cats with fluffy coats, sweet faces, waving plume tails and gentle ways.

Unfortunately, little of that luxury remains. But Persian artists were influential and admired elsewhere. One of them, Abol Hasan, must have liked Persian cats, for he painted them well. He was of Persian descent. His father had been artist at Isfahan's royal court before emigrating to Mughal, India. There Abol Hasan also became a court artist and two paintings of cats he did there have survived. They are now part of the Art and History Trust collection, often on museum display or tour. They can also be seen in the book *Art of the Persian Courts* by Abalala Sandovar—a smoky gray on page 342 and an orange-furred charmer ten pages later, both dated "before 1600." Both illustrate eleventh-century fables.

Surely earlier proof of Persian cat presence—paintings or written text—exists. Perhaps not. Fernand Méry, French authority on cat lore, wrote in 1966 that they first appeared in Italy in 1550, in France by 1600. Another source dates both European firsts for Persians as 1620.

Longtime researchers know that earlier dates for puzzling artifacts may often turn up in some long-forgotten letter or diary. Just such a discovery suggests that longhaired cats from Persia might have been known in Italy—or at least heard of— a year or more before Columbus sailed on his first Atlantic crossing.

LONGHAIRS IN OTHER PLACES

This clue came from Italy's wealthy principality of Mantua in the year 1490 when the fascinating and capricious lady known before marriage as Isabella d'Este was just settling into her role as a new bride. To make the palace feel more like home, she wanted pets and wrote a chatty note to her family about buying a lapdog at once and ordering a Persian kitten. Later another note mentioned she was expecting a kitten from Syria. Was this a real Persian? First ever in Europe?

Syria might have been merely the port of shipment, the kitten itself from Persia. It might have been longhaired. The fact that she wrote of *ordering* the kitten instead of just buying it immediately as she did with the lapdog, suggests that it was rare, but shorthaired cats had been known in Italy since the days of the Phoenicians. Will another lost letter explain? Or a forgotten painting?

In England longhaired cats weren't around till the nineteenth century. Owners began breeding Angoras to Persians hoping to get the best of both. Americans joined in and the chance of keeping either breed pure was almost lost. Somehow *angora* slipped into meaning "long, soft, silky" and was applied to goats, cats, rabbits and knitting yarn. The goats are actually native to the Angora area, but the rabbits were European mutants aided by human "engineering."

In the beginning, anyone who knew what to look for could tell Angora cats from Persian at a glance, even when both had all

COMBINGS SAVED TO SPIN INTO YARN SEEMED TO AMAZE EVEN THE CAT HERSELF WITH THEIR THICKNESS.

Holmgren photo

white, or all black, fur. Angoras had a narrower head, slimmer body, longer legs. Persians had a rounder head, somewhat plumper figure, shorter ears.

The first Angoras described by Europeans had all white fur and blue eyes. Later black Angoras with yellow eyes were seen. Still later, were accounts of white Angoras with yellow eyes, or one yellow and one blue eye. In contrast, the eyes of Persians, white or black, were gold to amber. The fur of either could be distinguished by touching it. The Angora coat felt silkier. Persian fur had more the feel of lamb's wool.

THE VAN CATS

By the late nineteenth century, all the changes caused by cross-matings had nearly done away with clear distinctions. Also, there was confusion due to those somewhat different longhaired cats found near Lake Van in the former Persian Empire (later in Armenia and now in Turkey) as borders changed. They were like Angoras in build, but had amber eyes. Furthermore, although they looked all white at a distance, at closer range you could see reddish areas on the tail, reddish cheek lines angling

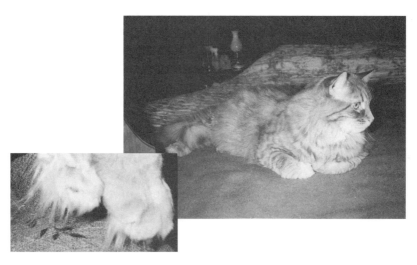

MAINE COON CATS KNOW COLD WEATHER AND HAVE TOE TUFTS AND THICK COATS TO MATCH BOTH COLD AND UNKNOWN ANCESTORS.

Joyce Petalunas

down from the outer corner of each eye and sometimes reddish splashes on the forehead. Later they would have any of the usual colors, and some European breeders today speak of both Turkish Vans and Persian Vans.

SAND CATS

Not everyone agreed. Zoologists had just learned of a wildcat species in the area with similar reddish markings over pale sand-colored fur. It was called Sand Cat and officially enrolled as *Felis margarita* in 1858. Individuals with some slight varying in shade ranged from Egypt to Pakistan in all-over reddish fur that matched the color of markings seen on a Turkish Van. Maybe Angora and Sand Cat had mated?

There was another question, too. Sand Cats didn't have coats as long as Angoras or Persians, but it was longer and thicker than the usual shorthair coat. They had long tufts of fur between the pads on the sole of each foot, a feature that had until now been found only on cats with long, thick fur associated with cold climates.

The tufts were especially valuable in winter when the snow lay deep and soft, with no hard-freeze topping. Anyone who had ever tried walking on such snow understood that the tufts would spread out like snowshoes and keep the cat from floundering. The tufts were especially long and thick on cats of the cold Russian steppes, and perhaps Persian and Angora ancestors had come from those northern lands. Perhaps they had come south with ancient Phrygians. Were Sand Cats also from the North? Here they were desert dwellers, so why did they have those snowshoe tufts? Travelers who knew the desert were quick to answer. Desert sand drifted as deep as snow. Steppe cats and desert cats had foot tufts for the same good reason: they needed them to survive.

MARGARITAS

Listeners had to agree. The phrase "survival of the fittest" as one of the principles of nature had not yet been heard when *margarita* was first enrolled. They had long since learned about animals that had whatever it took to survive and those that didn't. Still, they were puzzled when familiar animals began to behave in new ways or even look somewhat different—like the white cats with the reddish markings who really liked to swim.

In the cities—and especially in England—people with longhaired cats of unusual beauty were beginning to realize that they could sell kittens at fancy prices. Cats had always been exhibited at fairs and bazaars along with other pets, but now there were shows just for cats. Winning a First or Best in Show was worth it in satisfaction even if no money was involved. What everyone seemed to want most was a cat with the Angora's blue eyes and the Persian's sweet face and cuddly body. Now, more and more often, hopeful owners were dismayed at kittens that didn't have the best features of either parent. And all they could do was look at each other and wonder why.

IT'S IN THE GENES

As it happened, someone, an Austrian monk named Gregor Mendel, was already working on finding the answer. He was experimenting with crossing different kinds of garden peas, not cats, but the principles of mixed ancestry for animals turned out to be the same. By 1865, Mendel figured he'd done enough mix-matching to be sure of the conclusions. In 1866 his basic laws of inheritance were published by Austria's National Science Society, but they were generally ignored.

That was probably to be expected. Those who did glance at the title of Mendel's article must have shrugged and tossed it aside. Who cared about peas? You liked them or you didn't. Very few people, if anyone at all, realized he was talking about a lot more than peas in a pod.

Some thirty years later, three other Europeans who had been working on the same problem offered their conclusions for publication—and were told they were too late. They had confirmed Mendel's conclusions without knowing who he was or what he had written. Both agreed that with repeated cross-matings roughly one-fourth of the offspring would resemble the male parent and one-fourth would resemble the female. One-half wouldn't match either parent exactly, but would be like one another. Whatever new qualities they shared would then be passed on to *their* offspring. If the offspring would then pass on these features for four generations *and* all factors remained the same, the changes could then be considered permanent.

One of the three men went on to prove that changes could occur in individuals at birth without any cross-mating involved. He gave these spontaneous changes a name, mutation, from the Latin word for *change*.

In 1905, scientists found another term for the study of inheritable factors: *genetics*, coined from *genos*, Greek for "birth." Each factor then became a *gene*, a word intended for scientific use, but in time almost everyone was borrowing it.

By mid-twentieth century, genes were providing an answer to almost any question about the differences among cats—and other animal species—that anyone thought to ask. They also provided an answer for people who didn't really understand what genes were but didn't want others to discover their ignorance.

All that was needed, in this latter case, was an air of mystery, a shrug to disclaim responsibility and a know-it-all tone for replies of "Oh, it's all in the genes, you know!" or "Only the genes can tell!"

If the next question was *How do the genes know?* answering might not be so easy.

8

THE GENES HAVE THEIR SAY

Even today someone overhearing talk of cat genes might think the word was cat *jeans,* as in blue denims. Funwear for cats!

Someone really up on old-time slang might think it was just a mistake for that well-worn phrase of the 1920s—*the cat's pajamas.* It meant whatever was the latest fad or fashion, the most "in," of the inmost, the best of the best.

But genes aren't something that can go in and out of style. They are a part of each individual plant, animal or human from the first moment of life. They are too tiny to be seen without great magnification, but they are there, an actual form within a form. They are enclosed within an equally invisible threadlike fiber called a chromosome—like an undetectable grain of dust within another undetectable grain of dust.

The word *chromosome* comes from the Greek for "color" and "body." It fits, for the genes within this "color and body" hold the heritage of form and color passed down by every individual's direct ancestor known or unknown. The number of genes assembled could thus be beyond counting. All are there, but only a few are active for any one individual.

From ancient times people have noticed that babies, in barn, garden or home, may or may not look like their parents. One of the fun things when newborns arrive has long been pointing out each family likeness. "Has his mother's eyes," the talk begins—or father's chin, grandpa's red hair, Aunt Susie's nose. So the *fact* of inherited likeness is not new. But the why and how of the inheritance—the story of genes at work—did not even begin

BOTH JEANS *AND* GENES *INVOLVED?*

J. G. Francis, *Book of Cheerful Cats*, 1892.

to be understood by most people until well into the twentieth century.

In 1913, when the word *gene* was still very new, the definition was vague even in a medical dictionary. Not much to learn from "a transmitted germ of character," is there? Especially if you thought of germs as something that brought disease and you had to wash them off fast or else.

A few years later another text sounded more scientific but still didn't make the meaning very clear: "a hereditary unit in a chromosome." Expressing a scientific process or idea in ordinary terms isn't easy for the professional person who thinks only in the special language of science.

By the 1990s there were even more complicated terms and ideas involved. Besides active and inactive genes to explain there was also the presence of a substance called DNA (*d*eoxyribo-*n*ucleic *a*cid, the initials of its chemicals) that serves as the individual's identification tag, a Who am I? label provided by nature along with the genes.

GENETICS—THE RECIPE FOR EVERY LIFE FORM

For a moment, put these scientific terms aside. The way genes work can be explained with a more familiar comparison. Genes are much like the ingredients in a well-stocked kitchen cupboard. All sorts of seasonings and staples are there, but only a few will be used in each recipe. Only those that go into that one particular mixing bowl will affect the results.

So let's say there's cookie batter in the bowl when the phone rings. While the cookie maker is answering the phone an impish brother dumps in some odd ingredient just for a joke. Nobody sees him do it. Nobody knows it's there till the first bite. Then, what a surprise! Maybe it's a good surprise and everybody's happy. Maybe it's indescribably awful. Ichhhh!

Nature sometimes adds a surprise gene, too. Something that didn't come from any inactive ancestral gene but is brand-new for individuals of this kind. Once it is there it may be passed on to future descendants as readily as any inherited genes. It may be good, it may be bad—but it is always different. A change from what was already there. Science calls it a *mutant*, from the Latin for "change."

CREATING CATS—THE GENE MUTATIONS

Mutant genes have a very ancient place in cat history. Paintings of 1300 B.C. show that mutation had already brought areas of white (on paws, ruff, vest) to some royal cats. Other mutants didn't appear till cats and new kittens were familiar throughout Europe.

In 1979, a young British geneticist named Andrew T. Lloyd wondered if any mutant cat genes got their start in the Americas. He decided to search for an answer by making cat genes the subject of his doctoral dissertation at Boston University. Boston had been settled by English families and the first cats there had probably been brought from England. Now he would learn if their genes were the same as English cats or if mutants had been added.

He had studied about Mendel and his garden peas, of course. And while cats weren't quite as easy to study as a garden plant, he could see their coat color and length and general body build from a distance. No need to have them in cages. If he could get a good look at two or three hundred cats in each part of Boston and other nearby cities, he believed he'd have enough information for making reasonable conclusions. A survey of any kind, he knew, called for a representative sampling. Just checking a few cats wouldn't tell the story.

Eventually he would learn that he needed more time, more cats and a whole staff of cat watching assistants. But he enrolled at the university, talked with his advisors and started out on his own. Notebook and pen in hand, binoculars on a neck strap for closer check, he began ambling through Boston suburbs, peering into backyards and porches and playgrounds. To some Bostonians his actions looked suspiciously like those of

THIS LUCKY ADOPTED ORPHAN HAS INHERITED THE CHUNKY FUR
PATTERN OF THE ORNATA TO IDENTIFY ONE OF ITS WILD ANCESTORS.

Photo by Jenny Duchêne

a thief planning a heist—a problem he hadn't considered in his careful preparations. Most of the time a quick, polite explanation and the proof of his notes settled the matter. But one day a wary householder sent the police to do the questioning and he found himself cornered by police cruisers—three of them. Luckily the police accepted his story. Surveying cat colors was evidently too crazy not to be true.

When he realized he needed to do more than backyard snooping, he began checking cats in SPCA shelters and other animal-control sponsors with cats and kittens for easy study. With more help from these refuge cats and his own faithful crews, he would tally an amazing total of 6,500 individuals from thirty-five areas between New York City and various Newfoundland harbors.

He was especially looking for free-roaming shorthairs like those recorded in England. Shorthairs were the first cats in both Europe and the Americas, and were still more abundant than longhairs. The free-roamers can choose their own mates while housebound cats cannot, and therefore only those that roam represent a natural gene base and changes. Luckily he found all he needed. Finally, with a sampling of more than six thousand cats, he was ready to tabulate results.

Would he find the same colors and patterns abundant in England here in lands settled by Englanders and so give proof of genetic heritage? The answer was overwhelmingly affirmative. Similar genetic choices of color and pattern appeared in 99 percent of those 6,500 representatives of free-roaming American cathood from New York to Newfoundland. So high a percentage suggests that a cat-count walk in almost any North American city, east or west, might have similar agreement. At least a search through other suburbs and animal shelters to see if their color patterns also match those Lloyd named most abundant or most unusual, would be a challenge, especially if city founders were not mostly English. Lloyd, for instance, learned that New York, which was founded by the Dutch, had more black-and-white cats and fewer orange ones than cities settled by the English.

A TABBY BY ANY OTHER NAME

Genes in animals or humans take time to make a full impact, so the cats brought by early settlers have had more chance of making their mark. Early mutations also would have been like-lier to survive than newer ones. However, an overactive tom or one female can have considerable influence in a small area. So while any new cat survey may come close to matching Lloyd's eight or ten most abundant color patterns, there could be surprises.

Color, on any survey, comes first. Cats share a three-color base: red-orange (some breeders prefer red), black or white. This simplicity is complicated by the presence of a gene that dilutes the basic black or red to varying shades:

- Red-orange diluted produces pale orange, yellows, buff, cream.

- Black diluted produces grays, browns, tans.

- White and black may be solid color or appear in small irregular areas.

- Red-orange is seldom solid but will vary only in its own dilute shades.

Patterns—like colors—began with those of the African Wild-cat. It came in two colors, orange or gray, but a single pattern: dark striping on light background.

Dark lines on the body are thin and vertical, and broken rather than solid. On legs, chest and tail they are circular. The lighter color was either a gray lined in black, or orange lined in brown. More of the black/gray pattern reached Europe and is still the most common of all patterns among free-roamers. Britons dubbed it "tabby" and a dark marking of an M shape on the forehead is a pattern clue.

Today the lighter colors are so varied they are part of the label and Gray Tabby maintains a prevalence over Orange Tabby. A light gray may be called Silver Tabby.

THE TAIL IS SHORT, BUT A MANX IS NEVER STUMPED FOR WHAT TO
DO NEXT.

Photo by Jenny Duchêne

Mutation soon brought broader striping and coils, spirals, swirls instead of lines. For these the name became Blotched Tabby, as if it were a shameful mistake. It quickly became much admired, but the name remains a reproof for Nature's "error." The mutant pattern of black-and-white in irregular patches is called *piebald* as it is on horses. Black, white and orange is *calico* in the United States. *Bi-color* and *tri-color* also serve for these and all combinations. A blending of orange-and-black with pigment alternately banding each hair (not a patch) is *tortoise-shell* (no white). Solid color in any color or dilutant is also possible.

Along with these basic color patterns, Lloyd found four surprises:

1. **Manx** (tail absent or partial)   Nineteenth-century Britons chose the name because the first ones seen were on the Isle of Man in the Irish Sea. For top awards the tail must end at the rump with a hollow at the end of the spine, resulting in the nickname "Rumpie." Imperfect action of the gene results in a partial tail and the nickname "Stumpies." The mutation may appear with any color coat.

2. **Siamese**   The gene first recorded for cats especially cherished by kings of Siam, now Thailand, gives faded tones to body coat and limits darker colors to the extremities, called points. These are the face, ears, legs, tail. The first-known Siamese had dark brown points now called seal. A lighter brown, blue-gray, lilac-gray and other colors now appear. Kittens with only one Siamese parent are usually all black.

3. **Polydactyl**   The Greek word for "many digits" (toes or fingers) is used for cats with more than five toes on the front paws, or more than four on the hind feet. In 1876 it was reported by Dr. Gordon Stables of London in his book *The Domestic Cat* as an odd deformity. To him it was the sort of natural "error" that could happen to any individual, not something that could be passed on to future generations. Apparently most Europeans agreed.

4. **Maine Coon Cats**   These cats of unusually large size, long silky fur and an Angora-shaped head were first seen only in Maine, possibly before 1800. The raccoonlike black-and-tan tabby coloring of the earliest ones led to mistaking them for cat/raccoon hybrids. Maine Coon cats now come in all normal colors.

POLYDACTYLS APPEAR, BUT FROM WHERE?

Of these four, Dr. Lloyd discussed only polydactyls in his summary published in *Natural History* (July 1986). The others he omitted as found on common free-roamers only in one geographical area and on an occasional pet there or elsewhere. He had expected to put polydactyls in the same group, he noted, for he thought they were "conspicuously absent" from British and other European populations. But here in Boston he saw cats with too many toes to match the old "this little piggy" nursery rhyme almost everywhere he looked. How could there be so many when they were scarce everywhere else a counting had been made? When did the invasion of extra-toed cats arrive in Boston?

With the help of Boston historians he found an answer. Or at least part of an answer. In 1848—a really ancient date for American cat data—an Irish girl newly arrived in Boston wrote to her family in Ireland that six toes per cat foot was one of America's many oddities. Lloyd and his crew now began paying special attention to numbers of toes, and eventually reported that 15 percent of Boston cats were polydactyl. Extra-toed cats also existed all along the coast. On one, the toe count per paw was ten! But the farther he went from Boston, the fewer polydactyls were seen. To Lloyd there seemed one obvious conclusion. Polydactyly in North America started with some unknown Boston cat before 1848.

His conclusion went still further. He decided that the Boston mutant was the first of its kind in the entire cat world. Polydactyly had its origin in North America, a continent that had no cats at all until settlers brought them from Europe, he concluded.

Very possibly, it did. But that still leaves the extra-toed cats in London, described by Dr. Gordon Stable in 1876, without supporting history. Had they developed surplus toes as a mutant also? Or had one of them been brought from America? Obviously they hadn't had many English offspring to carry the mutant, or the mutant hadn't been as strong as in the first six-toed cat of Boston. Had someone in London decided the "deformed" ones with extra toes should not be allowed to have kittens?

No answers to those questions as yet. Nor to the statement published in New York in 1982, without details or verification, that the first polydactyl cat in Boston arrived there by ship. What ship? From where? When? The author, Leonore Fleischer, cited no source, gave no reason for not suggesting mutation as possible explanation.

Oddly, delving further into cat history may reveal that a claim for the first extra-toed cat may go to still another North American specialty: the Maine Coon Cat. Don Shaw, genetics editor of *Cats Magazine*, cites a 1950s census of Maine Coon Cats that showed 40 percent polydactyls, an amazingly high ratio! Did an ancestor come to America with extra toes and the other distinguishing features that make it a recognized breed? Or did the new genes develop here? No provable answers have yet turned up. Only homespun yarns of old-time Maine storytellers provide the coon cat saga. The only verifiable date to match the yarn-spinning is 1791. In that year in revolution-torn Paris, King Louis XVI and Queen Marie Antoinette tried to escape with their children. The plans were bungled and both Louis and his queen eventually died on the guillotine. But meanwhile all sorts of rumors about their plan were told, including one that insisted they had been offered refuge in French Canada. In preparation, then, they had sent on certain possessions with the loyal captain of a French ship Canada-bound. Six imported cats, just arrived from Turkey, were among the cargo.

By the time the ship neared the American coast, the captain may have thought being seen with the royal cats would brand him thief or royalist—either one a ticket to jail or the guillotine. At any rate, he was said to have turned them loose on the nearest shore, on the traditional dark and stormy night when no one was around to see the ship come or go, and the cats were on their own in Maine.

LONGHAIRS—HERE, THERE AND EVERYWHERE

Also verifiable is the fact that unusually large longhaired cats of close to brown-tabby pattern began to appear at one lone farmhouse or another. No farmer in his right mind questioned such a blessing; one varmint or another was always after his chickens,

THE NEW CATS FOUND A WELCOME AT MANY A FARMHOUSE DOOR.

Joyce Patelunas photo

and these brownies were fine ratters. By the time word of their arrival spread and farm families began comparing stories, there had already been kittens—probably several litters. And nobody could remember exactly when the first cat had arrived—or if there had been more than one, perhaps a mother with kittens. Sometimes the tales were only vague memories of what a parent or grandparent had said in years past.

Sometimes the story was of a Turkish sailor who used a cat, or several cats, to trade for food and supplies. Were the cats his own or Marie Antoinette's? Nobody was quite sure about that. But the word *Turkish* clung to whatever version was repeated.

Maine Coon Cats show traces of Turkish ancestry even today. That's Angora ancestry, of course, since the hilltop city of the ancient Phrygians was then a Turkish conquest. Look at the Mainer's wedge-shaped head—narrower than a Persian's—and at the longer body, tail and legs, the silky fur. Mainers, like the Angora, may be odd-eyed—one blue, one yellow. Like all longhaired breeds they have "snowshoe" hair tufts.

Similar cats mysteriously appeared in Norway. Now called Norwegian Forest Cats, their arrival has been credited to troll magic, far-sailing ancient Vikings or shipwrecked Turkish sailors.

So *Turkish* was a fitting word for cats a French queen prized highly. However, the French word for *Turkish* is *Turquois*. And since there are plenty of French-speaking people in Maine as well as over the border in Canada, someone in Maine might eventually have advertised the sale of a *chatte turquoise*—a Turkish female cat for breeding. Tourists who did not know the French language might well have stopped to see this colored wonder, found it already sold, and so went home to Boston or New York or Philadelphia with a story of Maine cats of the same blue-green coat as turquoise gem stones—unaware both cat and gems had their name from the country where they were first found in abundance, *not* their color.

Also possible is that the belief in blue-green cats came from mistaking a spoken *tortoise* for *turquoise*. Identifying orange-and-black fur as "tortoise" or "tortoiseshell" wasn't commonly done by people who didn't go to cat shows. Even cats with turquoise-colored eyes would have been something different, worth having. At any rate, people with cats to sell at fancy prices were still getting requests for blue-green cats as recently as a few years ago.

Another quirk in the tale is that some insisted the first cats were all white. Their kittens were tabby brown *after the mothers mated with raccoons!* Certainly the cats could have been white. Their eyes could have been blue in true Angora heritage. But cats and raccoons have such biological differences that, even

BELIEF THAT ANY ORANGE-FURRED CAT MIGHT BE THE SUN GOD IN DISGUISE MADE THE CATS THEMSELVES ALL BUT SACRED.

if they mated, no kits would result. Even more impossible is having offspring from such a mismating survive and have kits of their own. So we have to go back to the simpler story of genes at work and accept that the original cats mated either with each other or local farm cats. Their kits could have been white or tabby, with tabby the more likely color to be passed on to further litters. Any of the other colors in cat genes might appear, too, and today's Maine Coon Cats do indeed come in all the normal cat colors. The longhair and snowshoe foot tufts persist, and so some longhaired ancestor was certainly involved. The large size perhaps could be the normal result of living in Maine's colder climate.

But how did the extra toe count begin? Did it come with one of those mysterious Turkish cats perhaps meant for Marie Antoinette? Or did one of their descendants acquire the polydactyl gene there in Maine? And then did one of its six-toed descendants later head southward and pass on the gene to a Boston cat? Or did some six-toed roaming Romeo born in Boston amble northward to pass the gene to a Maine Coon Cat?

No answers to these questions as yet. Perhaps there never will be. There's only the "before 1848" date for Boston toes-plus, and there is no date at all for the first ones in Maine. Unless some written proof of extra toes in Maine Coon Cats before 1848 turns up, the honors must go to an unknown Boston cat, but not with clear title. If the extra toes were on those cats meant for the French queen, they arrived in Maine in the 1790s, well ahead of Boston's 1848 claim. And certainly long before Key West in Florida became famous for six-toed cats brought there in the 1930s by Ernest Hemingway. So an answer to the deciding question is still missing: When *did* a Maine cat first get that extra toe?

Also tangled in unprovable tradition is the matter of how cats on the Isle of Man came by their absence of a tail. Londoners had seen such cats or read about them in 1867, nine years before they counted extra toes. One Manx tradition claims a no-tail cat came ashore from a sinking Spanish ship in the Armada of 1588. Another holds one was brought by Phoenician traders before 500 B.C. Both are possible if that is a cat in a 1950 B.C. Egyptian sketch of a pet with stub tail found in a temple at Koptos and is now housed in London's Petrie Museum.

But there's no backing at all for the baleful and bloody charge that all Manx cats had full-length tails until Irish raiders began maiming every cat they could find. They'd sneak ashore, so the story went, grab any cat or kit they could find and cut off its tail so they could stick it in their hatband for a gleeful trophy. Adult cats soon learned to keep out of their clutches, but kittens weren't so skillful. So mother cats began biting off the tail of each new-born kit, and the raiding finally stopped. From then on, kittens were born without a tail—or with short stubs that offered no temptation—so stories claimed. No doubt Manx islanders and Irish mainlanders did raid each other's bailiwicks for booty in olden days. And hunters did take other tails, horns and pelts for trophies and wear them proudly. But a severed tail from a living animal could not be inherited by future generations. The genes pass on mutation, not maiming in which genes played no part.

Besides, cats were well loved in Ireland. A large stone cross outside a tenth-century church in County Louth shows a mother cat and kitten in loving embrace, both with tails intact. Cats were also valued as mousers.

Attitudes all over Europe would change by the 1500s, however. The belief that cats were creatures of the devil, companions of ghosts and witches, swept across the land like a plague. Killing a cat, torturing it, drowning it, mutilating it became an act of vengeance against evil—and for many Christians, against any religion that was not their own. Too many of those alien faiths had counted the cat sacred, told tales that gave it godlike powers. And cats, with their superhuman sensory perceptions, made such tales plausible as many a gory scene has proved.

CATS IN MYTH, FABLE AND WITCHERY

For Egyptians, the m'yaow was part of myth and legend from the beginning. First this creature had told them its name, and then their priests declared that the Sun god, their most powerful deity, had said he would take m'yaow form in fighting the Demon of Darkness. Each night the Demon in serpent form fought to turn the world to everlasting darkness, each night the Sun god fought to return, and now a chosen m'yaow would be at his side if needed.

Belief was easy. Their creed already held other gods and goddesses in animal form. And in Egypt where the sun shone all day, almost every day, with little rain except near Mediterranean shores, the dark seemed like world's end. Also, paintings of a golden-furred m'yaow attacking a huge and menacing serpent were now added to the Book of the Dead, which the priests prepared to place in each tomb. Similar paintings appeared on tomb walls. M'yaows readily attacked garden snakes and then, curled in a circle of sunlight, seemed touched with glowing magic.

Those that fought with the Sun god were males, of course, but Bastet was there as reminder that females also had sun power. Her picture was also on tomb walls, presented as a woman with the head of a cat. Clothed in a form-fitting, ankle-length gown with delicate panel design, she is completely feminine. Playful kittens at her feet proclaim her gift of motherhood.

Statues of cats were carved from wood or sculpted in various sizes in bronze to fit a temple niche or add to a casket. In the temples Bastet often carried an aegis, a symbol of her power, in one hand, while the other held a sacred rattle ready to send out a rhythmic beat of metal against metal. Both bear the tiny figure of

101

a cat. Some figures also carry a small embroidered bag over one arm as further witness to her concern for all womanly things. Other statues are completely feline. They may wear jewelry as beloved pets often did, one gold or silver earring, a neck chain perhaps studded with turquoise or enlarged to cover her shoulders. Seated, but head held high, her long tail curled in a half-circle almost reaching to the tips of her toes, she is truly a symbol of dignity and grace. Less often, the cat is lying full length, but still graceful.

SHINING EYES REFLECTING TORCH LIGHT OR FIRE GLOW SEEMED SUNLIGHT ITSELF AND THE CURLED CIRLE THE SUN GOD SHAPE— PROOF OF KINSHIP.

Sharbees.

Centuries later cats would also have a place in the myths of Greeks, Romans, Norsefolk, Orientals and almost every other people of Europe and Asia where live cats would eventually become pets. Later they would also have a place in fables, those pithy little lessons-in-disguise that most of us think began with a Greek storyteller named Aesop.

A MOTHER CAT'S TENDER CARE OF HER KITTENS WAS ALWAYS A REMINDER OF THE CAT GODDESS BASTET.

Sharbees.

AESOP'S TALE OF THE MOUSE WHO WANTED TO TIE A BELL AROUND
THE NECK OF EVERY CAT HAS ALWAYS BEEN A FAVORITE.

Aesop's Fabled Cats

Now it seems fables were told, written and pictured in Egypt by artisans at the Craftsmen's Village, as early as 1150 B.C. Aesop, if he ever existed, is said to have died nearly six centuries later, 564 B.C.

There is the possibility that the name was only an alias invented to hide the identity of a recognized Greek writer. This theory increases when we learn that no written copies of these fables were known in what should have been Aesop's lifetime— not written by anyone till after 390 B.C. Scholars trying to solve that mystery in the past have suggested that Socrates might be the unknown fablist. But remember that Aristophanes mentioned Aesop in his plays, had characters telling fables in Aesopian style and put cats on the bad-luck list. He seems a likelier candidate. The next versions were in first- and second-century Latin with considerable added material still credited to Aesop, and the name has been an alias ever since. The guess that its first user was Aristophanes is based on the possibility that the Greeks who stole Egyptian m'yaows also came home with some scraps of tales and sketches from Craftsmen's Village showing animals behaving—or misbehaving—in human style in order to deliver a message that would be read and remembered for its humor— and perhaps also for its lesson.

EGYPT'S ARTISANS

The Egyptian artisans may have thought of the idea or borrowed it from old folktales from Nubia. Nubians were there in the Village. So were Libyans and Syrians. But so many unknown animals from Nubian tropics were brought to Egypt as trade goods or tribute that the tales might have come with them. A favorite showed a cat driving off a flock of geese with gleeful culprit air. Since its companions are lion and fox, it may be a wildcat, not a m'yaow, but a take-charge pet such as the cat with the goose under Queen Tiye's throne might have suggested the plot.

Credit for putting cats in the world's first political cartoons goes to the Craftsmen's Village artists almost beyond doubt.

ARTHUR RACKHAM'S CAT IN A *1912* RETELLING HAS A VILLAIN'S AIR INDEED.

Workers there in 1150 B.C. were despairing at the luxury of the nobles and the poverty of their own village. Even food supplies—part of their contract—didn't always arrive on time. Actual revolt was impossible; the government guards were armed, no chance even for humble petition. But someone noted a parallel between their lot and that of rats compared to cats and set out to turn that imbalance topsy-turvy with cartoons of rats in regal elegance served by humble cats. The cartoons also featured armed mice attacking a castle held by cats! In other words, any scene with rats in charge and cats dutiful. Take an historian's time-lapse leap from Egypt in 1150 B.C. to England in the fourteenth century A.D. when retold Aesop's fables also gave cats the villain's role against both mice and poultry. The bad-luck label was known, too, and many a newly converted Christian felt cats were kin of the devil because they were sacred in pagan lands and therefore evil beyond redemption.

Good and evil were like white and black in their minds and so black cats were the most evil of all. When calamities occured, they blamed black cats and black-robed witches and imagined them flying together through moonlit skies on a broomstick, spreading disaster to humans below.

How did moon and broomstick get involved? Moon and magic (both good and evil) have always been paired. Old women always had a broom handy then. Besides, folklore had already made moon and a sky-sweeping broom a twosome. The moon was the farthest point eyes then could measure and reaching it became the symbol for the impossible. Reaching it by broomstick went beyond impossible to downright crazy.

TALES OF GOOD AND EVIL

Those who said "a man was off to the moon on a broomstick" were branding him a fool, simpleton, dolt, nincompoop. Nobody said that about the king and lived. So in London in 1415 when King Henry V set sail to tackle the French king's army—three times the size of the English troops—street singers expressed their opinion with this ditty:

There was an old woman tossed up in a blanket
Seventeen times as high as the moon;
But where she was going no mortal could tell,
For under her arms she carried a broom.
"Old woman, old woman, old woman," said I,
"Whither, oh whither, oh whither so high?"
"To sweep the cobwebs," she said, "from the sky.
And I'll be back with you by and by."

King Henry did come back—and as the victor! The French
had chosen to attack in an area too narrow to use all their troops,
and the Battle of Agincourt, October 25, 1415, became an
English victory. Street singers switched to a new song, boasting
the king had "plucked a hair from the pale-faced moon," and
the old song lost its meaning as it drifted into nursery lullaby
along with other tales eventually accepted as nonsense. A cat
was there with the old women on their broom-flight escapades,
probably because people remembered that the old Norse
goddess Freya had flown through the air riding a wildcat. Such
a picture had been painted on a church wall. Obviously, she
had made herself smaller or the cat larger for such a flight.
Another likeness showed her more comfortably seated in a
chariot pulled by two wildcats. They were too seldom seen to be
blamed for recent evil doings and so now the black housecats
rode beside witches on broomstick adventures in medieval tales.
They were not just cats, however, but ghostly spirits in cat form
sharing the witch's evil plans and therefore called her "famil-
iars"—able to curse you with the blink of an eye and steal your
soul with one eerie yowl.

An old woman living alone with no kin to give aid often cherished a cat as a dear friend and only companion. Cat and crone
were always together, the cat making play out of any work,
especially the task of trying to sweep the dooryard with a scrag-
gly twig-broom. Any villager hiding in the bushes to spy for
proof of witchery might see the cat pounce on the twig bundle
for a ride across the bumpy ground, and broom and cat be air-
borne for a brief moment of contact with a hidden rock. At that

very moment in a nearby castle another beloved cat might be taking the same playful ride on her lady's silken train as she crossed from window to mirror, with those close by smiling fondly. But there were no smiles on the faces of those spying villagers as they raced home to report proof of witchcraft in action.

Even in the seventeenth century in both Europe and the Americas, witches were treated more cruelly than any thief. Many were put to torture and an agonizing death, perhaps tied to a stake and burned alive, often with their cat in a sack beside them—or both in the same sack tossed into icy water to drown.

The horror of these deaths should be mentioned because it is part of cat history and human history. All that remains now of those old beliefs can fit pleasantly into Halloween just-for-fun pretense. Those witches and cats riding the skyway each October are only in our imagination. They are as we see them, all good witches and the best of cats.

CATS IN ART AND SCRIPTURE

As a matter of real history, quite a few people were trying to rescue cats from their burden of misplaced evil even in olden times. Christians were among those who now realized the truth. Cats were not slaves of the religions in which they had been sacred, not eager to destroy all other faiths. Cats were cats—the best mousers in the universe—and as ready to rid Christian churches of rodent ravage as they were in any edifice.

And what ravaging had been done! Both mice and rats had nibbled on altar cloths and priestly robes of every faith, gnawed sacred scrolls to unretrievable shreds. The only way to save what was left was to invite cats to take on guard duty.

As if in atonement for past disrespect, architects and artists in Europe's cathedrals and abbeys began adding cat scenes to their woodwork and stone sculpture for pillars, arches and choir stalls, to paintings for walls and prayer books and hymnals. Perhaps some who did so went home at night to tell their cats that the world was going to be a better place for them and all of cat kind. Storytellers also began weaving a place for good and loving cats into their versions of Bible tales, especially when their listeners were children with a good cat friend of their own.

Some of these stories are still being told and retold today in handsome picture books, each one with some small difference that comes with storyteller's privilege. A mother cat at the manger in Bethlehem brings her kittens to see the newborn Holy Child . . . or a scruffy-furred stray cat finds shelter in the innkeeper's stable and knows who the Child is and so hastily combs its tangled fur with teeth, claws and tongue so it will be fit to curl up by His side. Many a loving parent or grandparent must have told and retold this tale as a pleasant reminder for children to wash their own hands and faces so they, too, will be clean if the Christ Child should come their way

Some famous cat art pieces are still in churches and museums, or at least in books, ready to be found on a cat-and-mouse tour. Albrecht Durer painted a cat curled at the feet of Adam and Eve in the Garden. Several artists show a pair or two (different color patterns) waiting to board Noah's Ark. Jacopo Bassano painted several Ark scenes with cats, one of which is owned by the British royal family. One of Mary with the newborn Child at the manger, a cat at her feet, the ox watching from its stall,can be seen in the fifteenth-century cathedral of St. Omer at Pas-de-Calais in France or the book *The Cat and Man* by Gillette Grilhe. In cathedral cloisters at Tarragona, Spain, a two-part picture-story shows first a scene of joyful mice carrying a dead cat on a funeral bier and then a come-to-life cat jumping up to seize one of the pallbearers in its teeth while the others flee in hysterical retreat. Ghirlandajo's *Last Supper* has a darkly scowling cat huddled beside Judas—perhaps a suggestion that cats, with their extrasensory magic, knew long beforehand that this was the traitor.

In medieval churches with much carving on choir stalls, pillars and panels look for cats on any small space available— happy cats, mischievous cats, good mousing and rat-catching cats with proof of their skill in firm grip. Most of them are truly catlike, a hint that the artists actually had cats in the studio ready to serve as models for many a natural pose.

THE *M* THAT STILL MARKS THE FOREHEAD OF THE *AFRICAN WILDCAT* IS SEEN EVEN MORE CLEARLY ON MANY A TABBY-TYPE DESCENDANT.

Photo by Jenny Duchêne.

The great Italian artist Leonardo da Vinci drew cats by the pageful in his sketchbook, not all of them perfect, proof that cats with all their fluid movements are very hard to draw. Many of these cats are tabbies with the broken-line forehead M, which Christians of those days said came as Mary stroked its soft fur at Bethlehem. Islamites said it came from the touch of their prophet Mohammed. Ancient Egyptians believed it the same mark found on the shell of their sacred scarab beetle. Legends have a way of matching whatever the legend-weavers choose.

Along with all the many bad-luck omens that superstitions have given to cats, there is also the good-luck belief that each cat has nine lives. Why *nine*? Seven has been considered a lucky number, too, down through the centuries. If superstition alone were responsible, cats might be credited with seven lives instead of nine. But the number nine works mathematical magic no other digit can accomplish. *Multiply it by any other number and the digits in the answer will always reduce to nine.*

Nine, therefore, is the number of survival, and surviving is what cats do with magical skill. They twist out of traps and harnesses that would hold other animals firmly, land on their feet after falling from heights that leave other animals sprawled flat.

How? Not through abracadabra magic, but because feline anatomy is geared to flexibility. An unusually adaptable shoulder joint allows the forelegs to twist and turn in any direction, whether the rest of the body follows or not. A collar bone smaller than that in other species gives more room for this maneuvering, and all feline joints rotate on demand without dislocating easily.

Cats also display a determination to survive that seems to go beyond anatomy. They return to their homes—or follow their human family to new ones—after fires, floods, earthquakes or other disasters more often than any "law of averages" would seem to allow. How? For most people the only answer is that those nine lives come complete with a full bag of good luck.

BELOVED STORYBOOK CATS MAY MAKE THIS KITTEN WELCOME, TOO.

Sharbees.

People who don't like cats will probably mutter that the devil looks after his own. Even now in this hard-facts century some people still believe all cats are evil. To prove it, they describe the mysterious way the mere presence of a cat, seen or unseen, can start some people to gasping for breath, sneezing, choking. Others will be struck with sudden unexplainable terror. Removing the cat, or themselves, seems to cure instantly. Like magic?

Medics have a name for the affliction, if not the cause or cure. The Greek word for *cat* added to the Greek for *fear* produces a Latinized *ailurophobe*. People of the opposite opinion are *ailurophiles*—cat lovers. They sometimes remind the sufferers that people who fear cats must have been rats in some prior life—and they're not always joking.

Medical experts suggest that the breathing difficulties may be a reaction to the scent of fur or dandruff that most people do not feel. Some further explanation may yet be proven. Meanwhile, psychologists may probe for some forgotten childhood experience with a cat that led to panic. Recently, some have suggested that fear has been passed down through the genes of some unknown ancestor. So far, most geneticists believe that an ancestor's emotion cannot be inherited. However, fear of heights and other phobias have been cured by psychological treatment, and fear of cats may someday be conquered, too. Meanwhile, a good many ailurophobes are wondering why cats are becoming more popular than dogs. One practical reason is that landlords often allow cats where dogs are forbidden. Also, cats will use a litter box, or even a toilet if trained soon enough, and therefore do not have to be walked in all kinds of weather.

There's also the possibility that cats in read-aloud storybooks and nursery rhymes may have such a happy place in the family circle that some real little kittens with soft warm fur are welcomed and loved, too.

CATS IN FAIRY TALES AND NURSERY RHYMES

The first cats to appear in England in a printed book are from fables credited to Aesop. They were retold in English by the merchant-printer-scholar William Caxton of Westminster from his press in 1484. Printed books were still a new step in that year, and the book made its mark for history as well as for cats.

DICK WHITTINGTON

Honors for the oldest cat story of wholly English origin still in print go to the narrative of Dick Whittington and his cat, whose great adventures began around 1360. Dick himself was a real person with a firm place in English history. He came to London as a poor orphan, worked hard at whatever jobs a boy could find, served a merchant trader well, became a trader himself, was elected mayor of London three times between 1396 and 1419, was knighted by King Henry V and made a considerable fortune before his death in 1423.

Whether the cat he bought for a penny and rented to the trader as shipboard mouser really helped him earn that fortune may or may not be true, but it could have happened. Dick, in the years when he was Sir Richard, was said to have admitted that the cat brought him luck. Good ratting cats served on ships in those days. Perhaps Dick's luck came from seeing his cat's expertise and making sure cats of equal skill sailed aboard every vessel that carried his goods to foreign ports.

Also true is that similar tales of great rewards for ship cats are part of folklore in other seagoing lands from Denmark to Italy to Iran, for traders frequently reached ports where tame cats were not known. In 1699 English ship's surgeon and adventurer Lionel Wafer bragged of success in trading an English cat for Indian gold in the Caribbean and urged every sailor shipping out for the Americas to invest in a cat for good trading.

HOW MANY CHILDREN—GROWNUPS, TOO—HAVE CHUCKLED AT THIS CAT WHO, LIKE THEIR OWN PUSS, SPOKE FOR ITSELF.

By Wafer's day, Dick Whittington's story had been in print for nearly a century or perhaps longer. The little sewn-together penny paperbacks in which it first appeared were not dated and were soon read to pieces and thrown away. Some were surely in print well before the end of Queen Elizabeth's reign in 1603. The books were sold on street corners by vendors called chapmen; the word *chap* derived from *cheap*. The first chapbooks had only four pages. Later, some had eight or twelve, and often had a woodcut on the first page to catch the eye of possible customers. The chapbooks lacked names of authors or artists as well as dates, so there's no way now to honor the unknown craftsman who paid the tribute of letting Dick's cat speak for itself. There's the cat, pledging great ratting skill with a bold MEW neatly shown in a circle with dangling line just overhead. Is this the debut or a very early appearance of the dialogue balloon still used by cartoonists and comic-strip artists? Whoever drew it knew and *liked* cats.

Lack of author byline prevents personal blame for whoever first told of a half-starved young Dick Whittington making do with a grudging handout meal of dry crust and potato peelings. In his day there were no potatoes growing anywhere in England. White potatoes had their origin in South America's Andes Mountains, sweet potatoes in the Caribbean. Chapbook writers may not have known these facts, but modern writers are as free to correct the error as they are to change any other word in these hand-me-down tales. So shame on Joseph Jacobs, noted nineteenth-century folklorist, who added a note that potatoes didn't match the story's date but kept the peelings anyhow in the 1890s when he "cobbled up" (as he put it) one story from three old chapbooks. Author-artist Marcia Brown kept them, too, in 1990, but her illustrations well deserve the Caldecott Honor Book badge on the cover.

MOTHER GOOSE

Chapbooks were also first to have printed versions of the singsong rhymes heard in English nurseries since Queen Elizabeth's reign. Then suddenly, two centuries later, they were credited to a mysterious whoever with the name of Mother Goose. Cats, kits and pussies were all in these rhymes, so Mother Goose's story is cat history, too.

Who was Mother Goose? Two hundred years ago in Boston, the descendants of one Elizabeth Vergoose claimed she was the first to bear that name. She'd entertained many a child with her rhymes, even had some printed in a little booklet in 1719, they said. However no trace of that book or of anyone who'd seen it has ever been found. Even if a copy turns up, Mistress Elizabeth wasn't the first Mother Goose on written record.

In 1697 in Paris, France, more than twenty years before her verses were reported in print, scholarly Charles Perrault had published a book of eight French folk tales that he credited to this same remarkable fowl. On the right half of the double-spread title page was the formal title: *Histoires ou Contes du Temps Passé*—"Stories or Tales of Long Ago." On the left, a picture labeled *Contes de ma Mère l'Oye* identified this so-called goose as an elderly woman at her wheel, obviously spinning tales for listening children as well as thread.

Almost anyone in those days would have recognized the spinner as the traditional family nurse. The word now labels those who tend the sick, but then it named those who took charge of the family's children from birth to schooldays or even longer. Stories, songs, rhymes, maxims were always ready on her tongue for bedtime treat or to pass on a sugar-coated lesson on manners or morals. Sometimes a rhyme or tale might be made up on the spot. More often it was part of the nurse's own childhood memories, for village mothers and grandmothers did their own child-tending and storytelling. But upper-class families almost always had a full-time nurse in charge.

So Perrault's readers recognized the tales, but probably only a few of his fellow scholars understood the subtle aptness of his alias. Certainly he never explained his choice beyond admitting freely that he had retold old stories his young son had heard from his nurse. They had been told and retold for centuries, spreading from town to town, country to country, each new "spinner" adding something, omitting something else, using the folk-speech of the listeners. Now they were on a printed page with artfully polished phrasing from the pen of a scholar. Pens, in those days, were made from feathers, most often the long sturdy wing feather of a goose, its bonelike quill sharpened to a point. One day as Perrault's storytelling words slipped with ease from tumbling thoughts to quill tip it may have seemed the pen itself gave them birth.

"My goose quill their mother," he would have mused, pleased at the fancy. Suddenly he knew the perfect alias for these tales: *Contes de ma Mère l'Oye!*—"My mother the goose!"

Charles Perrault—obviously—was not the child of a goose or goose-girl. Nor had the tales been told by a goose herder. So

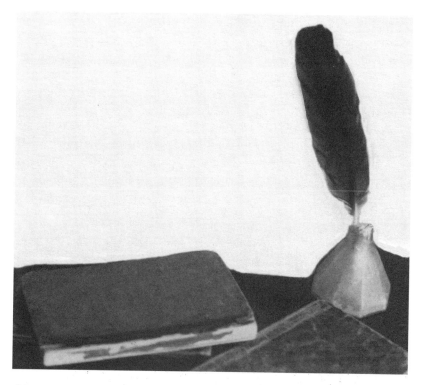

AUTHORS WHO WRITE ON COMPUTER KEYBOARDS WOULD HAVE
NO SUCH THOUGHTS—BUT WITH GOOSE QUILL IN HAND IT COULD
HAPPEN. COULDN'T IT?

fellow scholars and others who saw the name began to figure
out the solution to this odd puzzle. Being French, always
history-minded, they found an answer. That woman at her spinning wheel in his book must have been meant for long-dead
Bertha, the second wife of French King Robert the Second. She
had not been well liked at court and so spent much time at her
spinning—so much time that the foot so often on the treadle
spread out as flat as a goose's foot. Once court gossipers got
hold of that thought it spread far and fast, no longer whimsy
but accepted as fact. Bertha Goosefoot. Goose-footed Bertha,
they snickered. And by Perrault's time, some six centuries later,
the name was about all most people remembered.

Bertha Goosefoot, Mother Goose, triumphant puzzle-solvers
repeated happily to each other. Perrault was saying he had spun
new tales from old just as Bertha had spun new thread from

shorn fleece. It all fit so neatly that the riddle was forgotten—in France. But in England three other writers seem to have understood Perrault's wordplay and thought it well worth borrowing.

First to do so was Robert Powell, a puppeteer performing in St. Paul's Churchyard in London. The last playlet on his program in 1709 was titled "Mother Goose." No copy of the playlet has survived; perhaps the spoken lines came as needed to match an outlined plot. At any rate, there's no record of which of Perrault's eight tales was performed. Next to mark the feather was R. Samper, who in 1729 was only translating Perrault's title along with the tales.

Last was the bookseller and writer, John Newbery of London, who used *Mother Goose's Melodies* as his title for the most everlasting collection of jingles ever set down on paper. Of these three, he was most likely to have recognized Perrault's clue, for he was part of London's literary elite and surely heard others confess how the right words, after much pondering, sometimes came with sudden miraculous ease.

PUSS IN BOOTS

In French and English a favorite among the eight tales was the one Perrault called *Le Maitre Chat ou le Chat Botté,* "Master Cat or Booted Cat." Versions in Italy and Scandinavia and elsewhere also had this cat a boot-wearer, but let it turn into a fairy or an enchanted princess. For Perrault and Samper it was a cat all the way and Samper had the wit to call it Puss, then still a little-used foreign word from Asian lands and very old. Probably it was first used as Sanskrit *puccha* imitating a hiss but also with the meaning "long-tailed one." In other Far East languages it was accepted without special meaning as an imitation of the *psst* sound humans almost everywhere use to attract the attention of other humans or animals, not just cats. But it still has a feline bond as an echo of the hissing sound cats make in defiance and anger. In the language of the Aztec people of Mexico the word for the cats brought by the Spaniards means "little hisser," a diminutive of *mitzli,* their word for the lion-size *Felis concolor.* So cats named themselves in many a far land with a

long-forgotten hiss as they did in ancient Egypt with a plaintive mew-meow.

At any rate, Puss in Boots has remained the name through all the many retellings in English since 1729. For many, this finagling schemer makes up for his trickery with his valor and loyalty to the miller's youngest son. After all, turning a boy into a marquis and finding a princess for his bride takes a lot of doing. Reading it for the first time, one can only wonder *What next!*

The best illustrations for the tale, the best likeness of Puss himself, may be those of the French artist Gustave Doré done in the 1880s. From the elegant leather boots to a mouse trophy dangling from broad belt to the fancy feathers in his hat and the daredevil glint in shining eyes, Doré's Puss is superb. It has been copied often, frequently without credit. Some cat-loving readers prefer the illustrations of Kate Greenaway, Walter Crane or George Cruikshank. Most recently Fred Marcellino, winner of the 1990 Caldecott Honor Book award, adds a completely different Puss. He makes a literal match for his name by appearing only in boots and his own fur till the last page. Thus attired, he orders bewildered harvesters to join him in trickery with poise and pose that are both all cat and all conniver. What a cat! What a story!

Back in Paris in 1697 a neighbor of Perrault's, Madame Marie Catherine d'Aulnoy, decided honors for cats and conniving were also due the tale of a distinctly feminine rival, La Chatte Blanche. Madame, ardent feminist, felt she herself was the writer to put the story of The White Cat in print, and she had it and other tales ready for the printer in 1698. Her story begins with a touch of mystery—La Blanche was plainly not just a cat—and ends with a pleasing happy-ever-after royal romance that made it welcome at the court of Louis XIV.

However, it was too long and too cluttered with philosophical asides to maintain the spellbinding aura Puss achieves. Luckily a 1990 version by Richard San Souci is shorter and keeps the right fanciful touch, as do the illustrations by Grennady Spirin. Perhaps it will finally receive the applause Madame d'Aulnoy hoped for it and the other tales she called *Contes de Fées*, "fairy tales."

She did win a belated point over Perrault, though neither of them lived to know it. In 1750 when London bookseller John Newbery took over the Mother Goose alias for his own collection of English nursery rhymes, the bond between the imaginary befeathered author and jingly verse became so firm that Perrault's stories had to accept d'Aulnoy's title of French fairy tales. An American edition of 1945 still has that title.

Newbery must have been delighted with Perrault's pen name. The transfer wasn't new. *Goose* was a stand-in for *pen* in a far-older riddle jabbing at bureaucracy's endless demand for seal and signature by declaring the world ruled by calf, goose and bee. So Newbery took the alias without permission making his title *Mother Goose's Melodies* or *Sonnets for the Cradle* to mark that the rhymes were sung to old folk tunes. To lend prestige he added sixteen passages from Shakespeare without illustrations; but every rhyme had its small woodcut. A full-page scene opposite the title showed a woman reading to listening children and adults while a cat playing with a ball on the floor seems listening, too.

RHYME AND REASON

Perhaps one or another of the rhymes citing cats had caught her attention: Ding dong bell, the cat is in the well. . . . My kitten my deary. . . . Cat and the fiddle. . . . or

> *Great A, little a,*
> *Bouncing B.*
> *The cat's in the cupboarD*
> *And she can't see.*

A later version reads "The cat's a blind buff" for the third line and the picture shows a cat circled by children, sharing their game.

Every copy of that first little book of Mother Goose rhymes—just 2⅝" by 3⅞"—has long since disappeared, read to shreds

G<small>REAT</small> A, B, and C,

And tumble down D

The Cat's a blind buff,

And she cannot see.

a, b, c, d,

P<small>ERHAPS NO CAT EVER LET ITS EYES BE COVERED WITH A HANDKER-</small>
<small>CHIEF AS THE GAME IS PLAYED NOW, BUT THERE'S NO DOUBT CATS</small>
<small>LIKE TO JOIN IN ON WHATEVER IS GOING ON. THEY ALSO MAKE UP</small>
<small>THEIR OWN GAMES AND INVITE US TO PLAY.</small>

in loving hands. Its contents are known because an American bookseller-printer named Isaiah Thomas of Worcester, Massachusetts, saw a copy and happily borrowed it—woodcuts and all—for the first American printing in 1785. All copies of that edition vanished, too, but at least one copy of a second printing of 1794 was saved by the American Antiquities Society. It was reprinted in a special limited edition in 1945 thanks to publisher Frederic Belcher of New York City.

Many other editions, and other cat rhymes, followed this first printing. Whether called Mother Goose rhymes or nursery rhymes, they're still popular. Among the favorites for cat lovers are "I love little pussy, her coat is so warm" . . . "Pussycat, pussycat, where have you been?" But today's readers are often puzzled by the cat that ran away with the pudding-bag string. Cats chase strings, but pudding bags? Yes, *bags*. When most of the cooking was done on the open hearth, dough puddings were boiled, not baked. Patted into a loaf, the dough studded with plums or raisins was put into a cloth bag whose drawstring could be tied tight enough to keep the pudding dry during three hours or more of cooking in boiling water till done. The bag, emptied, washed and hung to dry with dangling string, was sure to tempt any cat or kitten. A quick snatch at the string tip and off goes puss, the bag flip-flopping behind. A substitute for this forbidden toy was often offered: a plump handful of soft wooly cloth tied in the middle with a string and wiggle, waggled along the floor by a human playmate. Far more puzzling today is the hey-diddle rhyme of the cat and the fiddle. Is it just nonsense, or a double-meaning jab at Queen Elizabeth I for tackling more than she could handle in sending English sea captains to become pirates and come home with Spanish gold? And was she also too daring in trying to keep the Spanish king a dangling suitor?

Letters written by her contemporaries establish that "cat" was indeed the code word for queen when gossip got too rough for plain speaking. "Cow" was also code for an important female, so Elizabeth is also challenged for her trying to "jump over the moon," a favored symbol for the impossible since the days when Henry V set off to conquer the French. That very story was in the introduction to Newbery's first rhymes, perhaps to remind

THE VIOL CLAIMED THE FIDDLE ALIAS FIRST, BUT THE VIOLIN SOON TOOK OVER THE ROLE IN RHYME, STORY AND EVERY-DAY USE.

adult readers that some of the following pages might also contain double meanings that nursery-age children didn't need to know.

In Newbery's version the little dog (one of the courtiers?) laughs to see such *craft*—not *sport* as in most present versions—and *craft* meant skill then, especially in trickery. Author Katherine Thomas in her book, *The Personages of Mother Goose*, makes it seem sly gossip, no match for just-in-fun nonsense. But her prying found a report that the queen would play a tiny fiddle and dance to her own tune when she was alone and things hadn't gone her way. "Fiddle" usually meant the bass viol then, but "tiny" clearly makes it a violin, not the larger instrument in Newbery's woodcut and some other volumes. At least the gossip adds to the cat-and-fiddle tangle.

Any reference to cat and fiddle might go back still further in English history and refer to antics at inns and taverns. A fiddle-playing cat has been pictured on signboards for such places since the days of William the Conqueror. According to actual records, an inn of that name belonged to a loyal Frenchwoman who had followed William to England. Her name, Catherine la Fidèle, sounded more like *fiddle* than *faithful* to English ears, and Cat was a familiar nickname. So merry-makers ready for a pint of ale said they were off to the Cat and Fiddle, and Catherine, being an astute businesswoman, ordered a signboard painted to match her new sobriquet. She must have prospered, for Cat and Fiddle inns and taverns still do business in English towns and villages.

Finding that piquant phrase on tavern signs in England's North American colonies isn't surprising. But one of cat history's minor—though challenging—puzzles begins with discovering a fiddle-playing cat in sedate Boston's most famous schoolbook, *The New England Primer*, by teacher and scholar Benjamin Harris.

Whether this feline fiddler was in the first edition out before 1690 may never be known. All copies disappeared long ago, literally read to pieces. It would be reprinted and sometimes

C

THE LESSON'S THE SAME
AND SO IS THE RHYME,
BUT WHAT MADE THE MUSIC
IN THE EARLIER TIME?

revised and a best-seller for more than a century, and some of these editions have vanished also. Those that do remain prove it the most solemn and serious schoolbook ever put in a child's hand. In homes it often stood on a shelf right beside the Bible, for it held Bible verses, the Lord's Prayer, Church of England hymns, Creed, catechism, and the still-used children's prayer, "Now I lay me down to sleep," with its grim reminder that death might come with no earthly awakening.

The puzzle begins to nag with finding that the rhyme to go with C in a picture alphabet in an edition around 1727 was cold fact:

> *The cat doth play*
> *And after slay.*

But the woodcut illustration and another in 1785 were make-believe fantasy. For the 1785 book the scene is a cat playing a violin for a happily dancing mouse, front paws waving. The 1727 edition pictures three mice, erect on tiptoe, prancing if not dancing beside a cat also erect. The space between them is just right for the missing bass violin, its former presence indicated by black spots where a cat paws would have plucked fiddle strings and the cat's chin rested on the finger board's scroll curve. Almost certainly the fiddle had offended someone, so it had been routed out of the wood block for the next printing.

Or perhaps instead of being offended, someone had objected to fiddling being the kind of "playing" that went with mouse murder. Now cats do look as if they're playing, having great fun, when they catch a mouse, toss it around and let it go to catch again. Actually it's Nature's way to make sure that cats practice enough to perfect their hunting skill. For kittens, it's a way to learn by watching their mother at work. Cats are born hunters, like all carnivores; their need for meat demands that they kill to survive. Even those fed by humans may not entirely lose that innate need to hunt. So there's no need to wonder why the play-slay rhyme was there to stay. The puzzle is why the picture didn't match the rhyme's meaning. Were fiddler and dancing mice there because editors liked cats and didn't want a bloody scene that would turn readers against them? Or because they thought children should not have such information part of a reading lesson? Or was it all a prank, part of the ill feeling between artist and editor that neither would admit?

One clue is that cat and fiddle have long been linked through the belief that the screech of a beginner's violin is firm proof the strings are made from a cat's guts. Listen to a courting pair in full voice and you might agree in the likeness between screeching strings and a cat's courting call. Actually, the strings have been made from animal guts—intestines twisted and dried in proper size—but from *sheep*, not *cats*. Nevertheless, a sheep's plaintive baa-aa just doesn't split human eardrums with cat-yowl intensity, and so the word *catgut* remains in use, adding its bit to cat conundrums.

Whatever else about cats comes up for questioning, pedigreed and stray remain welcome in many a family circle—including those at the White House.

11

PRESIDENTIAL CATS AND OTHER MEMORABILIA

Sir Isaac Newton, who died in England in 1727, is still considered among the most learned scientists of all time by many historians. Many also give special honor to his discovery that the earth's magnetic force holds the moon in its orbit. Few note that he also understood how strongly the moon lures cats to night roaming.

Newton's own cat must have made him aware of the attraction, however, for he added the invention of a swinging cat door to his other accomplishments. So Newton could sleep while his moon-struck cat went roaming and returned when ready.

GEORGE WASHINGTON

President George Washington and his wife, Martha, may have been first in the Americas to have such a convenience for their pet. Martha, so it was reported, was the one to order a door panel at Mount Vernon redesigned with come-and-go swing. What the president thought of the idea we do not know. It is very likely he agreed. There was plenty of room for safe roaming at Mount Vernon. No traffic hazards in those days.

ADAMS AND JEFFERSON

A cat door at the White House might have been out of the question, however, the Washingtons never had a chance to live there. Although the mansion's cornerstone was dedicated in 1792 as Washington began his second term, the place was still barely livable in 1800 when his successor, John Adams, decided to move in with wife, Abigail, in spite of hardships.

LIKE THE HUMAN FIRST FAMILIES, FIRST CATS CAME WITH AND WITHOUT PEDIGREE HONORS, BUT THEY WERE ALL SPECIAL IN THEIR OWN WAY.

No cats shared popular stories of the second presidential family or of Jefferson in 1801, or any of the other presidents over the next sixty years. Surely there must have been barn cats in all administrations. Even city families of means had their own horses and cow in those times, and perhaps chickens too. So there were lofts for hay and bins for grain.

WILLIAM HENRY HARRISON

Therefore there were mice and rats after the grain, and cats to keep the rodents under control. In 1841, when President William Henry Harrison took office, he made purchasing a cow one of his first duties. He chose it himself and helped drive it back to the White House. But no word of barn cats or house cats seems to have survived.

ABRAHAM LINCOLN

Twenty years later there were still cows in White House barns and still no mention of cats brought by Abraham Lincoln or his family. Lincoln did like cats, and dogs, too—so people who knew him well used to say. In the years after his assassination when the talk so often turned to Lincoln at any gathering, one of General Horace Porter's favorite tales was about Lincoln and the orphan kittens.

Porter had been General Grant's aide-de-camp the day Lincoln arrived to talk over a bloody battle. Three pitifully mewing kittens had just been discovered under the tent, the missing mother probably killed during the fighting. Porter looked at Grant, waiting for orders to dispose of them. Lincoln interrupted. "Here's one problem I can take care of," he said, reaching for the kittens. Opening the top button of his coat, he gently tucked them inside and took his leave. For Porter, the story ended there. He didn't need to say Lincoln kept his word. Any record of them after Lincoln's death has vanished, but his listeners knew the three were cared for, if not at the White House, then with a kind family elsewhere.

No cats were involved in presidential gossip as Andrew Johnson finished Lincoln's term; none in the eight years with General

CARING FOR THE UNFORTUNATE—PEOPLE OR ANIMALS—WAS A PART OF LINCOLN'S PHILOSOPHY THAT SPARKED MANY A STORY.

Ulysses Grant and his wife, Julia, at the White House. Toward the end of their stay, the press referred to Mrs. Grant as "First Lady" at times.

RUTHERFORD B. HAYES

The phrase caught on and so Lucy Hayes, wife of Rutherford B. Hayes of Ohio, was the first wife of a newly elected president to move into the White House knowing a title awaited her. Frequent and continued use by reporters, especially in society columns, made its usage popular all across the land. Inevitably someone would start using First Family too. But nominations for First Cat had to wait awhile, even though Lucy had always had cats.

On the inauguration day in 1877, the family cats were still back in Ohio where Lucy could be sure they were in familiar quarters and well cared for by friends. Lucy missed them and had to say so now and then. Newspapers picked up her comment and clippings reached the U.S. consul in Bangkok. David Sickels had been hoping for a tactful way to remind the new president of Siam's many needs. Now it struck him that a gift of a Siamese cat to a cat-loving First Lady would be the perfect opening—*if* he could persuade the king to agree.

To many Siamese people this was a royal breed, sacred, treasured by all and under the king's protection. It was bred only in the palace or Buddhist temple so the unique markings could be kept true. Some had been smuggled out, as m'yaows had been from Egypt long ago. Somehow a pair had reached England in 1871, but none had been seen anywhere in the Americas. Obviously such a cat in the White House was sure to set everyone talking and writing for newspapers as well as letters to friends, thereby giving Siam just the kind of publicity it needed. Of course the king agreed with Sickels's request. He even chose the little female himself and ordered full arrangements be made for safe journey. Sickels chose to call her Miss Pussy, and in the summer of 1878 Lucy received this letter, now preserved at the Hayes Presidential Library in Fremont, Ohio.

HOW "LITTLE SIAM" WOULD HAVE ENJOYED PLAYING IN THE CONSERVATORY WITH THE CHILDREN.

Rutherford B. Hayes Presidential Center, Fremont, Ohio.

Dear Madam:

*Having observed a few months ago in an American news-
paper a statement that you were fond of cats, I have
taken the liberty of forwarding to you one of the finest
specimens of Siamese cats that I have been able to pro-
cure in this country. Miss Pussy goes to Hong Kong
whence she will be transshipped by the Occidental and
Oriental Line, in charge of the purser, to San Francisco
and then sent by express to Washington. I am informed
that this is the first attempt ever made to send a Siamese
cat to America. I am,*

Very respectfully,

David B. Sickels

The cat arrived a little bewildered, but ready to be friendly,
and was promptly renamed Siam. Lucy was enchanted. The
entire Hayes family welcomed this addition to the bevy of pets
that now claimed the White House as home: two dogs, a goat
that pulled a cart for the youngest boy and a mockingbird that,
so Lucy wrote a friend, "deafened the house with its songs."
Evidently it also kept out of Siam's way, for there was no report
of friction. Quite the opposite for the family and for visitors.
"Siam Cat is growing daily in our affections," Lucy wrote in her
diary.

The exclamations at first glimpse were as much for the unfa-
miliar color pattern: pale body fur in contrast with deep tones
of dark and velvety face, ears, legs, paws, tail and the brilliant
blue of the eyes—unique eyes, not really crossed, but undeni-
ably slanted toward the nose yet somehow part of the cat's charm
for most visitors. Some, however, called them "squinty," and
some also thought the kink in her tail was not a beauty mark.
"If bred to our tom, what would the kittens look like?" people

asked. But they had no chance to find out. Siam had only a year at the White House before she became ill and died. No picture of her has been found. First Lady Lucy and family went back to Ohio. At the White House in the years after Rutherford Hayes, five other administrations had followed with no cat headlines. Of the next six presidential families, however, four were all in favor of cats.

Cat fanciers in London, were breeding Siamese now, and by 1895 a few were imported to the States. Unfortunately, most of them were a disappointment. The kittens often died soon after birth and adults were sickly, difficult to raise. Siamese were different in their needs, it seemed, as well as in their color pattern, and it took Americans a while to understand.

WILLIAM MCKINLEY

William McKinley and his wife, Ida, arrived in 1897 with a pet that was not only First Cat, but the first longhaired cat at 1600 Pennsylvania Avenue. Ida McKinley was an invalid and kept much to her room. The cat was always with her, and so most visitors had no chance to admire the beautiful long fur that went with her breeding. But the word spread that she was an Angora—the McKinley Angora, people said when they described the fur, or if they were friends, Ida's cat. No other name survived in general circulation until she had kittens and she became Ida's Mamma Cat.

She may well have been a true Angora with the wedge-shaped head and golden or blue eyes the Crusaders admired long ago. But Angoras and Persians had been crossbred so much by this time that few showed pure ancestry and the rounder Persian head was usually inherited. Most people then, except experienced breeders, didn't know the difference. Either term was used for any longhair. The McKinley administration ended abruptly with his assassination on September 14, 1901, and no more was said of Ida's cat and her "born in the White House" kittens.

TEDDY ROOSEVELT

For the next eight years the White House belonged to the animal-loving family of Theodore Roosevelt. Pets were shared by

ALL SIAMESE AT THIS TIME HAD THE DARK SEAL-BROWN COLOR AREAS AND ALL WERE KNOWN FOR KEEN INTELLIGENCE, BUT DID THEY REALLY LEARN TO READ? WITH OR WITHOUT GLASSES?

Photo by Jenny Duchêne.

the entire family, but the president claimed two cats as particularly his own. The first was Tom Quartz, a name borrowed from a cat in a story by Mark Twain. Tom Q and Roosevelt often played touch tag, a playful nip-the-trouser-leg affair. One day, however, it turned into *clutch* tag when the overzestful Tom refused to release his hold on the trousers of a visitor who was not amused.

Roosevelt's other favorite was a gray-tabby tom with white ruff and paws, a common color combination. Not at all common, though, were the extra toes: six instead of five on each front foot, five on the hind ones. Extra toes on all-white paws suggested the name Slippers, and both the president and his wife, Edith, felt special privileges were in order.

Slippers was a roamer. How far he strayed from White House grounds was never discovered. But he was a gourmet at heart and always came home for dinner when kitchen aromas told him a special banquet was in preparation. One night he was quite late and the harried kitchen staff hadn't the patience to serve his usual treats. With tail and head held high, he went where he knew the feast was being devoured—the state dining room. Familiar noises told him everyone was ready to leave. No treats here either! He crouched in mid-hallway, eying the door with reproachful gaze.

Here they came, elite of the elite—ambassadors, generals, cabinet ministers, titled diplomats from abroad, Washington officials of high rank—each with a beautifully gowned lady on his arm. The president and his lady guest led the way and he was listening so attentively to her that he almost missed seeing the huddled gray-fur figure. Now he caught the you-forgot-me eye-gleam and knew that moving was not on Slippers's mind. As skillfully as he would have signaled a dance partner, he led his lady to pause, gave Slippers a half-amused, half-rueful nod and then he circled his partner around and past the cat toward the East Room.

Behind them, the other partners had paused, too, and now circled around Slippers and down the hall. Almost any other

LIKE MOST PAMPERED CATS, SLIPPERS KNEW HOW FAR HE COULD GO.

group would have been annoyed or puzzled. But in the world of diplomacy, rank grants precedence, and rank was something these guests understood. They could read Slippers's message as easily as they did a fellow diplomat's raised eyebrows. The cat was asking due respect, or perhaps an apology.

Slippers got both. Even before all the guests had reached the East Room, the president was hurrying back to get Slippers and carry him to join the others. There on Edith's lap he held court so regally that even those who didn't care about cats were impressed. The story of a cat who knew his due and a president who understood hurt feelings was written for *St. Nicholas Magazine*, January 1908 issue, by famous author and philanthropist Jacob Riis.

WOODROW WILSON AND CALVIN COOLIDGE

Woodrow Wilson was the next president to have a cat, a white-furred beauty with golden eyes. Apparently it got little attention from the media. Calvin and Grace Coolidge had three cats—Blackie, Tiger and Bounder—who were seldom mentioned among an array of other pets, wild or tame.

HARRY TRUMAN

The cat that made the newspapers with President Harry Truman did not belong to the family. It was part of a publicity maneuver by an astrologist who hoped for an invitation to read horoscopes for the Trumans. So the cat somehow appeared in the White House yard, with the collar showing the address of his owner and the name Mike the Magicat, which led to his being sent home in the presidential limousine, but without an invitation to return.

GERALD FORD AND JIMMY CARTER

No one in those first years would have believed the liveliness of Chan, Susan Ford's perky Siamese, which shared White House years with the family of Gerald and Betty Ford until 1977. Surprisingly, the next First Family, Jimmy and Rosalynn Carter and daughter, Amy, would also include a Siamese. Amy supplied a musical name, Misty Malarkey Ying-Yang, and claimed for her the title of First Cat.

JOHN F. KENNEDY AND GEORGE BUSH

President John Kennedy's daughter, Caroline, had a cat named for her storybook friend, Beatrix Potter's Tom Kitten. After that, dogs, not cats, were presidential favorites, except for the two Siamese belonging to Susan Ford and Amy Carter. Dogs were especially in the forefront in the years when George and Barbara Bush were in the White House. When their dog, Millie, had her story "ghostwritten" by Mrs. Bush, it became a bestseller. Everybody knew about Millie then. Admirers used to marvel, certain no other White House pet had ever had such popularity—or ever would.

BILL CLINTON

But then along came the presidential campaign of 1992 and a particular, mostly black, white-pawed cat named Socks. Socks had begun life in 1990 as an orphan. A homeless, nameless orphan abandoned with his sister on a doorstep in Little Rock, Arkansas. A neighbor who tried to find them a home was a piano teacher. Her pupil due for a lesson that day was Chelsea Clinton, daughter of the then governor of Arkansas and his wife, Hillary. Chelsea had been grieving for her much-loved Cocker Spaniel, recently killed in an auto accident. Now a little white paw reached for her hand and Chelsea felt instant bond.

The all-black sister was appealing, too, but both Chelsea and her mother were drawn to the brother. Chelsea named him Socks and he moved into the governor's mansion with an air of knowing he was meant for a life of superior status. When Governor Bill Clinton was named Democratic candidate for the presidency, Socks became convinced of it. Photographers were always around now, making do with Socks if the family wasn't available. One day five clicking cameras at once were aimed at the cat, and when a sixth appeared he faced it with a challenging meee-owwww. Cameraman Mike Nelson must have chuckled as he clicked again. Couldn't have got a better pose if he'd been able to talk cat and say "pretty please" in meowese.

Socks

SOCKS SOMETIMES PAW-TOE-GRAPHS HIS PICTURE.

Courtesy of the White House.

Everyone who followed the campaign knows how Socks made news, story after story, photo after photo. Socks walking with Chelsea on the other end of the leash, Socks in Chelsea's arms, Socks looking supremely smug. You couldn't help thinking he'd known from the beginning just how the vote would go in November. Maybe nobody voted for Bill Clinton because his daughter had such a cooperative cat. But Socks certainly kept the voters reminded of just who was on the Democratic ticket.

After the election a cartoon of Socks at the White House became an easy way of taking a crack at the president, jokingly or otherwise. They were so popular that two fast thinkers registered a Socks the Cat trademark. Often he was shown with an official First Cat seal beside him—even on the end of his litter box. Inside the White House he had the run of the East Wing by day and slept in Chelsea's room till he felt at home.

Pet stores and souvenir shops began offering all sorts of goods for Socks fans. Small statues, mugs, paper-cutters, T-shirts—even one with a picture of Socks and the label "Move Over Millie!" She had her book, but Socks had a video game. There were even souvenirs for the sister, adopted and named Midnight. If geneticist Andrew Lloyd happened to see any of this array, he might have reminded buyers that some token of New York City would be appropriate, too. Black-and-white is a predominant color pattern for cats in New York City, as it was for cats in Amsterdam, before Netherlands folk emigrated to what is now New York. So the unknown ancestors of Chelsea's cat could have come from Manhattan Island and their ancestors from Holland.

Toe count, however, suggests that another ancestor likely came from Boston, the home base for polydactyl cats in the Americas. If Socks could give his opinion on the matter, he'd probably say that Little Rock is ancestry enough to keep track of. He doesn't need a stream of long-lost relatives turning up to ask him for shelter. One cartoonist actually showed him ignoring such a petitioner. Descendants of Slippers, also with Bostonese extra toes, might check in for Socks kinship, too. Tracing their claim would be next to impossible, though, the way Americans have been moving around the last one hundred fifty years.

When you remember that there were no cats anywhere in the Americas until Europeans brought them, the idea of checking your area for the first records of house cats might be a project well worth following. Would you guess that in the year 1877, the same year that Consul David Sickels thought of sending a Siamese cat to Lucy Hayes in the White House, no housecats of any kind lived in the frontier town of Deadwood, South Dakota? At least that's the story.

A TOWN WITHOUT CATS

Many another western town was without cats then, too. And new settlers from the East used to shake their heads—and possibly utter a few fervent oaths—as they recalled how hard it had been to find someone to take the new batch of kittens their old cat back home used to produce each spring. They'd never thought to bring a cat with them. Too much bother and impossible riding in the coach on a train. They'd find one wherever they decided to stay . . . .

They chose Deadwood, where there were no cats to be seen. Every time a wagon train with supplies came through they'd ask the driver if he knew anybody with good mouse-catching cats to sell. Never thought they'd have to pay for a cat. Weren't rats here, but every other kind of hungry little varmint was always ready to gnaw open a flour sack. A lone miner thought he had enough flour for flapjacks and hoe cakes to see him through, but those gnawers would chew themselves a backside hole and munch away before he even knew they were raiding.

As long as there were just complaints, none of the drivers listened. But when miners started talk about paying—and the only money they had was gold dust or nuggets—a driver loading up for Deadwood took a chance and was ready with every cat and kitten he could find. What happened next might be told in several versions but you can picture it this way: "Cats for sale!" he called out as he pulled up in his usual place in Deadwood. "First come gets first pick. Get yourself a good ratter while they last!"

They didn't last long. A miner out at his diggings had sighted the trader's wagon and hurried to rouse the town. Now they were all here and eager to make a deal, with gold dust ready for a cat and flour and whatever else they could afford. Suddenly there was just one scrawny old gray cat left but it had a wary eye and would likely prove a better mouser than the pretty little tabby that had sold first. Or so the driver said. And several buyers agreed, for the price went up as each one tried to outbid the others and it went for twenty dollars! At least that's what the driver said when he got back to the nearest city. And the word went out to drivers and settlers: take a cat with you if you're heading West.

Somehow nearly everyone had forgotten that "No cats!" had been the word from Columbus and early Spanish settlers long ago . . . and later settlers in Virginia and the Bahamas and New England and Canada and every other part of the Americas. By 1971, when a plea came for cats to help rescue rat-plagued farmers in Colombia, most North Americans who heard the report on NBC's *Today Show* thought it must be some crazy out-of-season April Fool joke. How could there be any place without cats?

Very easily, it turned out. Small towns and inland areas in Colombia had never had many cats. When rodents invaded a village, the one or two cats there couldn't handle the attack. Villagers asked the government for help and were sent chemicals that killed the cats and didn't affect the rodents that had already built up immunity.

So cats were sent, and follow-up stories explained that the rodents were not only destroying grain, they were also biting anyone who tried to stop them—especially children—and infecting them with a new and deadly disease. There were also a few reports from medical aides sent to check on a plague in India. Towns there with cats did not have the plague—nor did they have many rats.

STRAYS AND THE LAW

Here in the United States, however, the complaint in both towns and cities continued to be the abundance of unwanted strays. In some cities there was a movement to abolish free-roaming cats altogether. Require cats to be leashed and licensed, people said. In 1949, Illinois bird-watchers had tried to make that state law, but then-governor Adlai Stevenson vetoed the bill. Not because he liked cats better than birds, he wrote in explanation. But for cats, birds were natural food; roaming and hunting were natural behavior. Small birds, including the Illinois state bird, the beloved cardinal, were also natural food for hawks and owls and other predators in fur or feathers. Most of the small birds were predators themselves, killing insects and worms to feed their young. Hawks and owls, like cats, killed rodents and so rendered the community good service. Stevenson felt the state should not deny liberty to any of them.

Perhaps no state will ever pass a leash law for cats. After all, that would apply to cats in every farm and village, as well as in cities. And leashed cats can't do needed mousing duty. But some cities are attempting leash laws or licenses as one good way to reduce the number of unwanted strays that must eventually be euthanized by local officials. Another way is to make a smaller license fee for cats that have been spayed or neutered. To be fair, perhaps an exception should be made for older cats who might not easily learn new ways and are not the menace as hunters that younger, more agile cats undoubtedly are. Also, a reasonable time limit must be set before penalty is exacted. Most cats, and most dogs, need a little time to learn how to adjust to a leash or to staying inside, using the litter box, giving up familiar roaming. Many cat owners who are also bird-watchers have already found a way to help their cats adjust to indoor living, perhaps with a screened patio or window ledge to ease the strain.

Anyone who can ease the burden of destroying surplus cats deserves a place on the cat lovers' honor roll. One name to enter is surely that of TV's Bob Barker, who manages to add a plea to the audience to spay or neuter their pets to every broadcast. Save room also for the nameless volunteers who donate time to compare cats in animal-shelter cages with notices for lost cats in the newspaper and notify possible grieving owners. The overworked shelter staff seldom has time for this service.

Cats don't always get the hero praise dogs earn for saving lives, but they do in Greenville, Pennsylvania. People there still talk about the cold winter night Ned Marini's gray tiger-stripe cat, Boots, rousted him out of bed with banshee yowls and frantic dashing up and down stairs, bedside to front door and back again.

"Get up! Get out!" was his warning, plain as any smoke alarm.

Ned obeyed, rousing his family with shouts of "Fire! Fire!"

No fire in sight, but Boots was still at the door and the Marinis looked out to see the house next door about to burst into flame as the whole family—parents and five children—still slept. Shouts and pounding soon wakened them and they all got out in time as two hunting dogs in their kennel yard at the far end of the lot began to bark at gathering neighbors and fire trucks. Boots, so friends recall, held court for several days as townsfolk came to offer praise due.

Some years later and half a world away, praise was also given the cat in the Dutch embassy in Moscow, who heard the faint hum of a spy's bug hidden in the embassy wall. No human ear could hear it, but the cat pawed and whined till someone investigated. Restless actions by other cats have warned of earthquakes, tornados and prowlers. Cats also sense human sorrow and are ready to give comfort with soft paw touch and purr, even to strangers in a nursing home. Some cats lack the self-confidence needed for such visits, but those who have it are treasured guests.

A cat story that is merely amusing—no heroics involved—may be especially welcomed by listeners of any age who are not able to have cats of their own but wish they could. Cat tales make a scrapbook for gift times, too, or a tape for nonreaders. One to include is the tale of the cat whose real name was Duke but earned another after it did moonlight prowling around a house occupied by U.S. Secret Service operators. All sorts of security devices were on duty, of course, and one monitor kept showing a mysterious blip, night after night. A very slippery spy, obviously. No footprints. No traces of any kind. Who was he—or she? What secret was worth such persistent snooping?

THE ONE YOU LOVE IS BEST.

Kaseberg photo.

A top agent called in for conference looked at the monitor. "Kind of crazy pattern," he offered. "Anyone around here have a cat?"

A quick check of a new VIP neighbor with impeccable clearance revealed the night-wandering Duke, thereafter referred to as Blip (plus a couple of uncomplimentary adjectives from disgruntled spy hunters).

Also worth retelling is the story of the Oratorio Ghost, alias the Phantom of the Chapel. On the University of Chicago campus the chapel concert choir was rehearsing Bach's Christmas Oratorio. Suddenly, just at a brief pause for a solo voice, there was an eerie interrupting trill.

Was someone playing a joke? Or was a rejected applicant trying to make trouble? The next night, at the same pause, the eerie trill came again. And again the night after that. But the person that went with the voice couldn't be found. The mystery might have remained unsolved. But the soloist needed to leave early one night. Hurrying into the hall she saw a cat waiting patiently by the door for someone to come along and let her out.

"Mee-oww?" the cat asked in that familiar trilly voice, and then gave a tail wave of appreciation for service as her camouflage orange-and-white coloring blended into the shadows, and another as the soloist laughingly sang her cue notes.

Some people, hearing her story, would ask what kind of cat she was. The answer usually came with a shrug: "Just a cat. Just another stray."

For any proud member of a cat-breed club, that reply stirs up a scornful look of disapproval. Maybe a lecture. For them there's no such thing as just a cat. "Household Pet Cat" is one term used by cat show people. There are over thirty others identifying recognized breeds. Still others for varieties, patterns, colors and other terms people who care about cat differences might want to know. People who want to breed cats or "talk cats" with breeders have to know them, or at least know they exist.

The Cat Fancy! What a flippant phrase—for pedigreed cats and the people involved in breeding and showing them in award-winning competition.

The word *fancy* came to English from the Greek *phantasy*—an eerie illusion, something imagined. About three hundred years ago it got tangled with *fanatic* and its slangy offshoot *fan*, both expressing biased enthusiasm, and *to fancy* thereby gained the added meaning of "to like," "to prefer." Naturally people liked the best and so *fancy* eventually became the word for anything of high quality, above the ordinary, elaborate, not plain. Gradually it came to mean something done more for pleasure than just earning a living.

Raising cattle or wheat was plain work. Raising pet cats and dogs or racing pigeons and roses was fancy. Those who did so were fanciers. All more than a little roundabout but still reasonable.

FROM COUNTY FAIR TO EXHIBITION HALL

Dog fanciers were having their shows in London by 1850. Cat fanciers were still keeping to country fairs and church bazaars, not daring big-city splash. But in 1867 when Charles Ross of London published his popular *The Book of Cats*, describing several breeds and color varieties, other cat fanciers realized London was ready for them, too. They took time enough to do it right and the first professional cat show opened at London's fashionable Crystal Palace exhibition hall.

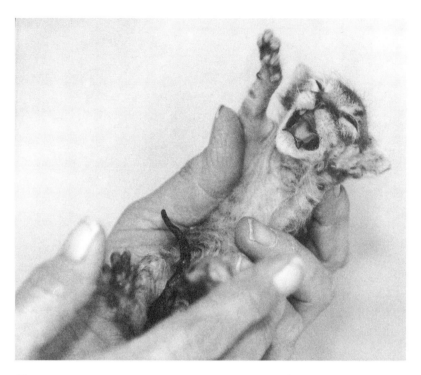

FROM NEWBORN KIT TO FULL-GROWN CAT THERE'S PLENTY OF WORK—
SOMETIMES GRIEF—AND WITH LUCK, JOY.

Photo by Jenny Duchêne.

Both the elite and the just curious attended. After all, Queen Victoria was known to be very fond of cats, especially her Blue Persians. And anyone who had read Ross's book was eager to see all the breeds he had described. His admiration had been mostly for Persians and Angoras, the three-colored Spanish cats with black-white-and-orange fur, or rare blue cats exiled French monks had found on their wanderings. He thought the tailless Manx cats "measly looking," but people wanted to see them, too. No doubt about it. The Cat Fancy had arrived in England.

Four years later Scottish fanciers opened their first show in Edinburgh. Paris hosted the first French exhibit in the 1890s. News of all the to-do roused envious fanciers in the United States and Canada. The first real cat show on this side of the Atlantic was held at Madison Square Garden in New York City in May of 1895. Chicagoans made their splurge in 1899, Canadians in 1906.

Britons and Americans organized more shows and clubs. The more shows were held, the greater the need for established terms and rules of procedure. The first attempt had come in 1889 in the book *Our Cats* by fancier Harrison Weir of London. Much argument followed and in 1910 the Governing Council of The Cat Fancy of Great Britain ruled that every cat shown there must have its pedigree registered with them, not just local cat clubs.

The United States, with its larger territory to cover, had two registries, American Cat Association started in 1906 and Cat Fanciers Association in 1908. Now there are several more, including the International Cat Association, all with numerous affiliated clubs and frequent shows. Dates and places for shows, the addresses for registries and clubs and other information of interest to the Fancy appear monthly in such magazines as *Cats*, *Cat Fancy*, and *I Love Cats*.

FOR THE RECORD

A registry keeps the pedigree record of each cat enrolled so that it can be verified if the cat is sold or enters competition. Also on record for each breed are the Standards required—the body structure and other features that must (or must not) appear if a show prize is to be won. These Standards must be easy to see and recognize by judges and owners. They usually involve hair length, body length and shape, leg length, shape of head, eyes and ears. Color of eyes or coat, or special markings (color points, white paws) may also be stipulated. British Standards usually include coat color. In the United States color indicates a variety, not a breed, except in show categories.

The color pattern called Tabby used to be considered a breed mark, but it is now seen on many breeds (even Siamese color points) and so is rated a variety. It has long been explained as coming from the dark-and-light broken striping on wild ancestors and changed through mutation to wider swirls or blotches, but always a dark-and-light contrast. The name Tabby marks that contrast and is generally accepted as coming from Attabi market in Baghdad, once famous for its two-tone silk.

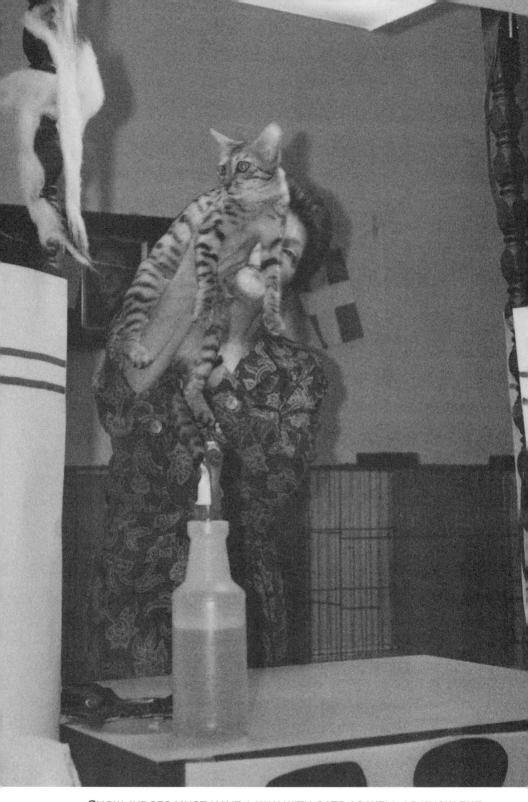

SHOW JUDGES MUST HAVE A WAY WITH CATS AS WELL AS KNOW THE
RULES FOR EACH BREED.

Sharbees.

EVEN AFTER FOUR THOUSAND YEARS, TODAY'S KITTENS SOON SHOW THE MARKINGS ONCE CALLED "SHIN GUARDS AND WRIST ARMOR."

Photo by Jenny Duchêne.

Some people think it is an abbreviation for Tabitha and so make Tabby a nickname for female cats to match Tom for males. Tom is sometimes credited to a popular storybook cat of 1769. There's a chance, however, that both Tom and Tabby stem from Ta-myy, that far older Egyptian name for a m'yaow of special importance.

In today's Fancy terms, Tabby is sometimes limited to a cat with *libyca* striping. Others choose only the blotched swirl patterns. However, it may include all two-tone patterns—any color, any breed, either sex.

This multiple usage gives tabby cats a special place in cat history because the two-tone coloring, rather than pattern shape, gives evidence of both *libyca* and *ornata* ancestry. So do the

THESE THREE OWE THEIR CURLY HAIR TO A BARN-CAT ANCESTOR IN OREGON BORN WITH A PERMANENT WAVE IN 1982. IN 1995 THEY HELPED WIN CERTIFICATION FOR A NEW BREED, THE DALLES LA PERM.

Photo by Jenny Duchêne.

circular bands so many cats today still wear on forelegs and haunches. One early classifier, unaware any Latin label was already on file, made these bands the identifying mark of the African Wildcat: *Felis ocreata maniculata*, "Catlike One Wearing Shin Guards and Wrist Armor." Less scholarly English folk made the same comment with "booted and gloved." White paws, however, were usually responsible for the gloves. The boots might have been influenced by a certain boot-wearing fairy tale Puss.

DESIGNER GENES

The Cat Fancy, through the registries, takes responsibility for establishing general terms and rules and defining the Standards by which each breed is judged at cat shows. They also decide, by official approval or rejection, which new breeds qualify for admission to a registry or which features can be added to breed Standards. The first demand is that the new breed or feature be well established, not just a one-time novelty with no proof it will occur regularly in succeeding generations. Such proof takes a formidable amount of time and patience.

Rules may change from time to time, but usually proof of a new feature's continued appearance over three or four generations is required. Perhaps only one kitten in the next litter will inherit the change. New mates might be tried to test whether it is the male or female parent carrying the gene, or if it came with the kitten. Breeders sometimes try mating the dam to one of her male offspring when he is full grown, or the sire to a grown female, or grown siblings to each other, one of which shows the diagnostic feature, or to some healthy, handsome nonrelative.

If the new feature or breed is documented enough in healthy cats, the registry may put the request for approval on a waiting list so at least the new name is on file for priority. Registries these days may have forty to fifty accepted breeds on record and two or three hopefuls waiting. All in all, establishing a new breed is never an overnight success and often fails.

Creating new cat breeds by intentional design is considered a recent fad by most people. But it really began something like four thousand years ago when Egyptians chose to honor their

Sun god by only having pet m'yaows with sun-colored fur. Since the wildcats had gray coats too, not all kittens were the wanted color and gray ones were given away or disposed of somehow—perhaps as temple sacrifice, perhaps sold secretly to some eager foreign trader and thereby making gray-coated cats more abundant than orange ones in Europe.

Today's designing can be done with all the knowledge science has provided over those four thousand years. But that doesn't mean it's all according to fixed rule. There are still many surprises.

THE CASE OF OLD BREEDS AND NEW DESIGNS

TWO FROM TOMB AND TEMPLE

Two breed patterns besides tabby striping inherited from *libyca* and *ornata* were seen on cats in Egypt's tombs and temples. One now belongs to the Abyssinian and the other to the Egyptian Mau. Both would be first known to British fanciers by other names.

The *Abyssinian*, now fondly called the Aby, first drew attention from Londoners in 1868 because of the unusual speckled coat. Each individual hair is like every other from nape to rump—dark at the tip with lighter bands down below. "Ticked," countryfolk called it, meaning lightly touched, and soon learned it was found on rabbits and squirrels and other small furry wildings the world around. One of them is an *agouti*, a rabbity-ratlike species from Central and South America. Oddly, modern geneticists prefer to call the pattern agouti instead of ticked, but no one in London in 1858 knew that. Along with the ticking, they could see a dark streak down the spine, faint rings down the tail to the very dark tip plus a hint of tabby leg armor and the traditional M on the forehead. So it was a kind of tabby? A ticked tabby or a ticked shorthair?

Anyone who knows that *Felis chaus* is Africa's only wild felid with ticked coat may offer a different answer. Both the *chaus* and the Abyssinian have long pointed ears, which *libyca* and tabbies lack, and could not have contributed to the Aby gene pool. M'yaows had the small size *chaus* lacks. If the two mated when they were together at Bubastis, their kittens might well have matched the Aby in pattern and size.

TICKED FUR IS NATURE'S HIDEAWAY CAMOUFLAGE AND COULD HAVE
COME TO THE ABY BY MUTATION OR AN INHERITANCE FROM THE
JUNGLE CAT.

Klinger photo.

However, a new pattern may become a mutation. Wildcats of slightly varied patterns once ranged all down Africa's east coast, following Egypt's Nile to Lake Victoria and the Blue Nile to Abyssinia, now Ethiopia. They have been long ignored as *libyca* subspecies, distinctions forgotten, but one could have had ticked fur. The cat Londoners saw in 1868 could have been a natural breed. Either way, ticked fur—and curiosity—are a nondebatable part of its heritage.

The Aby's right to the Abyssinian name, however, is disputed by those who believe the cat in London was London born; had never known the African land the Greeks called Abyss Country because of its high rocky ridges and deep chasms. Was the Aby, then, first to be named for a land it had never seen and no ancestor ever knew? Had geographical accuracy been shoved aside for a word with glamour?

Abyssinia had glamour for Londoners in 1868. British troops had just returned from a victorious expedition to rescue British citizens imprisoned by King Theodore in that rocky realm. General Sir Robert Napier, commander of the British army at Bombay, had sailed with forces battle-ready for the Egyptian port of Zula on the Red Sea at Abyssinia's northern border, was given map and guide by the consul and marched south. A rugged 420-mile trek lay ahead before he could reach the king's castle-fortress at Magdalá where the British prisoners were held. Both members of the diplomatic staff and missionaries were among them, some recently taken, others there for more than four years. Napier had sixteen thousand men. The king had less than a fourth that number, and he was also threatened by attack from rivals for his throne, so there was small doubt of a British victory even in hazardous unknown terrain. Still, the fighting was hard, and there were British casualties. Theodore, seeing the strength of both the British and his rivals, called for a truce and told Napier he would surrender. First, however, he asked Sir Robert to take young Crown Prince Alamayahu with him lest he be slain by someone aspiring to the throne. Napier agreed, put the teenager in the care of an aide, and waited for the formal surrender. Instead, Theodore took his own life.

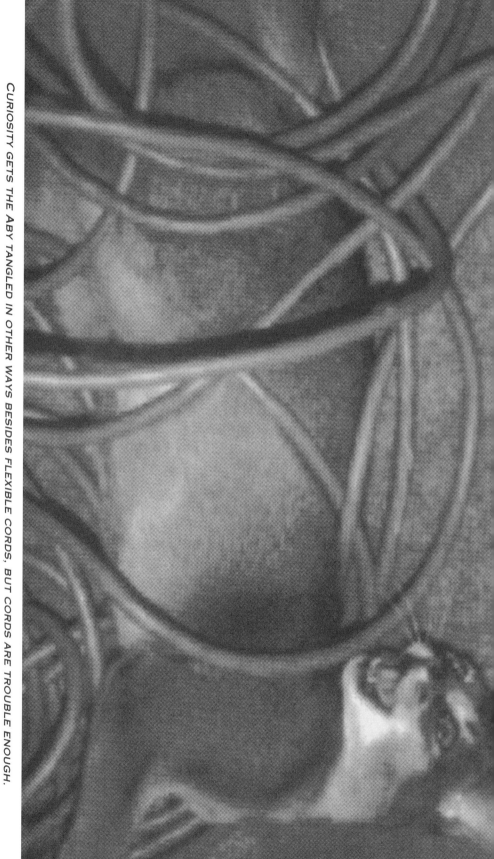

CURIOSITY GETS THE ABY TANGLED IN OTHER WAYS BESIDES FLEXIBLE CORDS, BUT CORDS ARE TROUBLE ENOUGH.

Klinger photo.

Napier—with troops, freed captives and royal refugee—made prompt return to Zula and ordered further voyage back to India or England. Was a certain ticked-fur cat among those who reached London? Was it perhaps the one thing Prince Alamayahu could not leave behind? Or had some member of the expedition or a prisoner found a furry friend? Had it been bought in the market at Zula instead of coming all the way from Magdalá? Or was it already there in London and the prince, seeing it, would welcome it as a friend, saying he'd had a cat of that very color? Or was just all the fuss about Abyssinia enough reason to make any London kitten a namesake? Someone might even have remembered that to ancient Egyptians the country called Abyssinia had been part of Nubia, the homeland of many of their wild pets.

Any one of those suppositions might be true. All that seems certain is that a ticked-fur cat was in London about that time. If it belonged to the prince he would have had to find a care-taker, for Sir Robert had kept his promise and enrolled the lad at Rugby where cats were not welcomed. Sadly, the prince died within the year and whoever had the cat would probably have kept it. Was that a certain Mrs. Barrett-Lennard who is reported as the cat's owner in some older texts? It was a female known as Zula, and the name of the port where Napier's ships anchored was another glamour word in London that summer. Whoever had this cat first sold it to someone who knew breeding and had found a faintly marked tabby male that might help preserve the ticked pattern. That, at least, is a fact, not question.

HISTORY OF THE FANCY

For the Fancy, breed history begins with official registration, and the first ticked-fur cats on register in London were males presented by Sam Woodiwiss, owner, who declared them of the same "unknown" parentage, one born in 1892, the other in 1894 and bred by a Mr. Swinyard. ("Unknown" may have meant not registered.) Registry names such as Silver, Aluminum, Salt, Platinum and Quicksilver over the next fifteen years suggest their color beneath the ticked top was grayish rather than the reddish-gold hue that later was preferred. Careful breeding also faded much of the darker tabby markings.

WHOEVER DESIGNED THE MOST GRACEFUL TEMPLE STATUES MUST
HAVE HAD ABYS POSING AS MODELS.

Klinger photo.

Two ticked shorthairs of British registry were imported to the United States in 1907. One was named Aluminum, the other Salt. Others with a more rufous tint came later and some American-born Abys in the 1930s had an even rosier glow. By 1988 they were registered as Red Abyssinians. British cats now needed their color tag, too, and ruddy became an accepted term. Most British breeders still prefer just this one color. But U.S. fanciers have already established several hues and more may follow. Color has its place in Aby history, but ticked coats, curiosity and a physique to match the grace and elegance of bronze temple cats will always define the Aby best.

Ticked fur without the Aby conformation, however, can define a new breed. Cats who carry this gene due to possible *chaus* ancestry have been seen in Singapore streets for years and were ignored as if dark hair tips were a flaw caused by their gutter life-style.

Finally, someone who knew about the Aby saw the possibility of what could happen with careful breeding and household companionship. Soon designer-made kittens were winning friends at home and abroad. Official registration as the Singapura (the native pronunciation of Singapore) came in 1988. To compare it with the Aby look for a more rounded head and a blunt tail tip.

So the Aby remains the Aby. Those who know it well declare it is always and completely itself. Those who know the Egyptian Mau are likely to claim similar aura for this other cat with an ancient history not everyone is ready to believe.

THE MAU

The name *Mau* is clearly one of several alphabetical answers to the old hieroglyphic riddle of owl + quail – chick = M W with the missing vowel supplied by reader's guess. Obviously it must match the cat's voice and in English the rhyme would be mow, maow, or meow. But in Italian the most likely vowel choice would be *au*.

As it happens, Mau did come to the cat Fancy records from Italy. The woman who submitted it was a Russian who had been living in Italy most of her life: Princess Nathalie Troubetskoye. Her family had fled Russia when the nobility were no longer welcome, and in 1950 she was living alone in Italy except for friends. Among them was the Syrian ambassador to Italy, who helped her to get a cat that also had royal heritage and was in a land not its own. "This is Lula," the ambassador would have introduced them, holding out a sleek, silver-furred cat with shimmering sea-green eyes. "Let me tell you her story."

The princess may already have known the story of Egypt's prized cats, but she would have been too polite to say so. As she listened she stroked the soft fur and must have thought how much the cat's story was like her own. Here in Italy both had been welcomed, but both had problems. The ravages of the Second World War had left no place for either of them. She had not yet found the kind of life that satisfied her, and cat shows were not able to offer the big rewards of more prosperous eras. During the war years there had been little food for humans. Starving was as much a threat as bombing and cannon fire. Many people had to sacrifice their pets to euthanasia rather than watch them suffer. Cats, dogs, even canaries left homeless might find a stewpot waiting. There was no time, money or heart for cat shows when the war was over, even if pedigree records and cats had survived.

Only a few of the pedigreed cats were available, and Lula was one of them. Nathalie asked herself, "Would there be shows with awards worth the high cost of daily care?" Not soon in Italy, but perhaps in the United States.

Did the ambassador make the suggestion or did the princess think of it for herself? They had talked before about the possibility of her going. Now here was a way. Could she take this cat—and a mate—to the States with her? Could they be her investment for a beginning, a way to make her dream of success in a new homeland come true for herself and the Mau, too?

Much talk surely came before action, but the ambassador offered to write to a friend in Cairo asking for a good male for

MAU KITTENS STILL WEAR THE SAME SILVER FUR, THE SAME IMP-OR-ANGEL LOOK.

Sharbees photo.

Lula's mate. After a wait that must have seemed like forever, a male named Gepa arrived. Like Lula he had sea-green eyes as shimmery as translucent jade. Like Lula he had pale gray fur with darker markings. Both of them were happy to have a mate.

The kitten Nathalie decided to keep was a little silver female, soon named Baba. This is the Russian word for grandmother, and perhaps the princess chose it as hopeful omen of a time when this little one would be grandmother and great-grandmother to a long line of kittens as lovely as herself some-where in faraway America.

Whether that was her dream-wish or not, it came true. Baba—when she was old enough—was mated to an Italian male of another line named Gregorio and their first son was named Jo-Jo. Gregorio was only borrowed to add his genes for variety, but the other four belonged to Nathalie and sailed with her to the States in 1953. They carried both color genes of *libyca* and *ornata*—buffy orange with black/brown markings or gray with charcoal, which would be known as "bronze" and "silver" by the Fancy—but had the chunkier striping of *ornata*.

Soon she had a cattery with the exotic name of Fatima to attract customers. Acceptance by the Cat Fanciers' Federation came in 1958. Now she began entering shows and one of the "grandchildren" won best silver Mau three years running, 1971 to 1973, making the name of Fatima's Ula one to remember. In the Canadian Cat Association she became a grand champion. The cattery continued for several years and the last litter sent to the CFF was registered in March 1979. Today breeders and registries still have cats whose pedigree could contain the name of the little grandmother Baba and the others who made silver the favorite color for the Egyptian Mau in America.

For ancient pharaohs, the favorites had to be those of the ginger-and-cinnamon coloring now called bronze. Only that sun-touched hue would have produced the belief that the cats were the symbol, even the incarnation, of Ra the Sun god and his shining golden orb. Almost every cat in tomb murals has this coloring, proof enough of its superior value. So color and pattern prove that Mau ancestors posed for these historic scenes.

Cats of the same coloring and pattern were known in Italy at least as early as 79 A.D. That was the year when the great eruption of rumbling Mount Vesuvius buried the nearby city of Pompeii so deep in volcanic ash that its ruins weren't discovered until 1748. There among tumbled walls and tragic proof of disaster was a mosaic, still intact by chance of fate, picturing a young cat with a captured bird, perhaps its first successful hunting trophy. The artist clearly showed the difference between unbroken bars on legs and chest and the interrupted body lines.

Tiles could have been chipped to show leopardlike rosettes and rings if any had been there to copy. Instead there are marks, stylized but still enough like those on today's cats to show that this one, too, had African Wildcat or its next-of-kin Indian Desert Cat for ancestor. The cat that posed for the mosaic may not have been the direct ancestor of the Maus that sailed to America with Nathalie Troubetskoye, but both had ancestors on Egyptian murals.

Today's cat Fancy regulations urge breeders to strive for round spots, not broken lines, on their Mau kittens. Spots are apparently thought romantic or exotic, lending a touch of the wild. The cats themselves don't always agree, and few nicely rounded rosettes and rings appear. The same contrariness appears on the Mau's British counterpart. This puzzler has been well known in Britain at least since 1889 when it was shown in London under the misnomer of Spotted Tabby. British fanciers quickly realized its broken marking was not true tabby type and decided to get by with the name Spotted Cat, Spotty for short. It wasn't popular and had almost disappeared by the time American Maus changed cat history. After some delay the British Fancy decided not to recognize the Mau as a breed and changed the name of its rival to British Spotted Shorthair.

THE BRITISH SHORTHAIR

Now began the mating of British Shorthairs to Siamese to gain a bit of the latter's slender body and wedge-shaped head but keep Shorthair colors. For the Spotty this resulted in a new breed: Oriental Spotted Shorthair. Actually, the first Maus in America had a slightly wedge-shaped head. Had it come with some

*SPOTS AREN'T LEOPARD ROSETTES, BUT THEY AREN'T TABBY STRIP-
ING. HEAVILY MARKED BACKBONE IS INHERITED FROM ORNATA.*

Sharbees photo.

wartime mismating in Italy that had gone unrecorded? Was it a
mutation? There are no answers for either of those questions—
or the question of what will happen to the Mau or Spotty. Also a
riddle not yet solved with firm agreement is the relationship of
certain shorthair cats in blue.

THE BLUE-WHO? A RIDDLE

Blue coat colors, like gray, comes with the presence of genes for
both black and a dilute (gray is a dilute). When there is also a
lack of strong red (orange), the resulting gray will likely have a
bluish tinge. Whether the tone should be called bluish gray
or grayish blue may be open to dispute. The cat Fancy has
decided on one label: blue. Due to the meddling of fancier

THE TWO COLORS OF THEIR ANCESTORS STILL BELONG TO DESCENDANTS OF LIBYCA AND ORNATA.

Sharbees photo.

manipulations "blue" is already part of the official name for over fifteen varieties. Only a two-gene get-together is needed.

Nature, it turns out, did some meddling first. Five breeds once recognized as unique all have fur of Cat Fancy blue: British Blue Shorthair, Russian Blue, Chartreux, Maltese, and Korat. The slender body and long legs of the Korat, a Thailand native, and the Russian Blue (along with other differences) keep these two as unique. Each is a natural breed that has been kept true to its natural conformation. But what about the British Blue? Is it the Chartreux under a new name? And was the Chartreux also known as the Maltese?

THE MALTESE

Although facts aren't clear, the Maltese may have been the first with a blue coat. Malta is an island is the Mediterranean just south of Sicily where east and west sea trade routes meet. Over the centuries its harbors were known to Phoenicians, Greeks, Carthaginians, Romans, Saracens and, in the sixteenth century, Christian knights. The French under Napoleon took it from the knights in 1798 and the British annexed it in 1814, releasing it to self-government in 1914.

Phoenicians and Greeks reached Malta first with cats to trade, and Phoenicians took them even farther—to Spain, where black cats would be famous for their glossy coats. So there could well have been black cats on Malta before 1 A.D. and, when the genes were willing, a black she-cat could have had blue kittens. Because the island was small and cats were few, the same parents might have produced other blues or the kittens would have mated when they were grown, and the color became established.

Sometime in later years, perhaps as late as the 1790s when French revolutionists were ousting religious orders, Carthusian monks fled their charter house near the Chartreuse Mountains in southeast France and took refuge at various monasteries elsewhere. When they returned in 1816 they had blue cats with them, sturdy creatures with the full cheeks and powerful jaws that still mark the African Wildcat. The Island of Malta was one of the places where exiled monks had found shelter during the Revolution and since other travelers would tell of blue cats from Malta, the island also seems the source for the cats that became known by the monastery name of Chartreux. (The monks were already famous for Chartreuse liqueur that has a greenish hue, and so the blue cats got the masculine spelling.)

THE CHARTREUX

Chartreux cats were seen in England as early as 1867. Charles Ross called them "blueish-grey . . . not a common color . . . esteemed as rarities." In 1889 Harrison Weir wrote of them as "definitely French" while other blues were Spanish, Russian or from Malta by way of America.

Londoners who kept up with their reading could have known about those Maltese cats much sooner. An 1857 news item told of a New York merchant who had sent for a whole cargo of Maltese cats from the island of that name. They were quite the rage for awhile, but by 1903 they were reported in *Dick Whittington's Cat Manual* as "shorthaired blue cats known as Maltese cats which used to be extremely popular in America." Perhaps their fading charm was due to fading of blue to gray as the cats were left to choose their own mates. Even in England the Russian Blues mated with Chartreux or British Blue too often and a purebred Chartreux would be decidedly scarce till after World War Two. The Maltese, meanwhile, had been dropped from British Fancy records—or perhaps had never made official standing in the first place.

THE RUSSIAN BLUES

Russian Blues needed considerable help from breeders to regain original form after wartime mismatings. A plush double coat is this breed's most distinctive feature. This was the result of cold Russian winters and a reminder that an ancestor was the pet of Czar Nicholas I in the early nineteenth century. Long legs and long, slender body separate it from British Blues and drew attention when the cats first arrived in England on ships from the port of Archangel sometime before 1880 when a Russian Blue made its debut on a London show bench.

For a while they were known as Archangel cats, but Russian Blue is now the official label for international use. Russian Blues in Britain or Sweden may be slightly different from those in the United States.

THE KORAT

The Korat arrived in England in 1896, last of the blue coat riddles to be shown in Europe. Because it came from Siam it was labeled Blue Siamese on the British show program, but viewers who had long been assured that all Siamese had slanted eyes and precisely patterned coat colors could only stare in disbelief. The cat on display had eyes that were definitely round and its coat was all-over grayish blue. Renamed for a district of its homeland, it was allowed to face the public with eyes and fur that might have come from *Felis ornata*.

In Siam (Thailand) there had been no question of its place of honor. In comparison to the other Blues, it is not as ancient as the Maltese, but it is no newcomer to catdom. A long-cherished manuscript in the national library at Bangkok proves it has been known and honored in Siam for more than six centuries.

The writing is poetry—nineteen carefully penned tributes, each for a pet who deserved praise for the good luck it had brought its owner. Among them, some are of Korat blue to prove that six-century heritage. Each verse is written in traditional Thai pattern—two columns side by side, four lines each, all with the same number of syllables. Because most Thai words had only one syllable, no space was left between the characters. So to modern readers it seems a poem of eight words instead of eight lines and not easily read. We accept the librarian's promise that full honor was given and that Korats are still counted good luck.

As a guard against spoiling that good luck by crossbreeding, the Thai government refuses to let a Korat cat leave the country except to reliable breeders who have promised it will be mated only to its own kind. Silver-blue coat, green eyes and a heart-shaped face are the cherished marks Thai cat lovers hope will never change.

Insisting on such strict regulations has come about in part because of all the changes that have come to other historic breeds, especially the Angora and Persian, as fanciers continue to "design" new breeds from old.

DESIGNING BRINGS DANGERS AND DELIGHTS

Redesigning the prized longhairs began in the nineteenth century before the word genes was well known. People wanted their Persians to have blue eyes, or their Angoras to have more cuddly bodies. They thought mating one to the other might grant these wishes. The Persians did get blue eyes in time, but Angoras of pure strain all but vanished.

A century later Nature did some designing of its own and a mutant Persian with a pushed-in Pekingese-type nose appeared. Anything different was the breeder's goal and suddenly Pekefaced Persians were the fashion, the prize winners. Others had to follow suit or lose both sales and awards.

As a result, the nose retreated still farther and cats began to have considerable trouble breathing. In addition the jaws no longer meet and the face has taken on a chinless pout that hardens the sweet face that had first won Persians their following. Even worse, the pushing has preempted some of the space occupied by the brain, giving Persians a reputation for stupidity. Luckily, some breeders did not follow the trend and we still have sweet-faced, intelligent Persians to maintain original high standards.

The Angoras, after World War Two, could be found only in their original homeland, and not many even there. Hopeful Turkish fanciers kept looking for a healthy unrelated pair, plus one or two more to vary the gene pool, and found them at the zoo in Ankara. Breeding began, succeeded, and so the ancient city on the hilltop has double reason to claim these slender beauties as its own. Breeders there agree that the name Angora is too well known to give up, but ask that it be Turkish Angora. Making the change on official records is in process, but getting it into everyday speech may take a while. At least Turkish breeders had enough full-quality adults to share them with breeders in England, the United States and Canada by 1960. By the 1990s the honor rolls of grand champions were once more including Turkish Angoras. Now there are kittens for sale with descriptions such as "Playful cats of regal bearing and ancestry."

Soon designers were trying to turn every available shorthair into a longhair with persistent cross-mating. Their success indicates that hair length is easily changed without natural mutation. A thicker fur aids survival in cold-weather areas and thereby increases the potential number of individuals to pass the gene to others. So, then, did one or more Angoras with this gene follow northern nomads south to the hilltop city for which they would be named? Winters must have been cold there, for wild goats at Ankara and camels near the Caspian had heavier coats than others of their kind elsewhere.

Did the cats near Lake Van acquire the longhair gene through mutation, or by mating with Angoras? The two share several features Persians do not have. And did Persians get their different coats by mating with *Felis manul*, the wildcat with the longest, thickest fur of any small feline? The skulls of these two are not identical, but they are both broader than those of other species. Both have ears wide set, both have the chubby body, short legs and dense undercoat that Angoras and Vans lack. The Sand Cat, *F. margarita*, also native to the area, may have had a *manul* ancestor to give it wide-set ears and broad head too. And *margaritas* may have shared their red-fur genes with Vans.

Did later Angoras sail with Turkish traders and leave descendants in Maine and Norway? Some day, genetics may provide answers. For now the question mark still looms darkly.

The oddest design came by natural mutation in 1966 in a Canadian barn-cat litter. There it lay, squirming and mewling like the others, but not a hair visible on its body, nary a whisker on its chin. "Naked!" came the gasped exclamation of disbelief. "Hairless!"

As the kittens grew, the family and visitors saw other differences. The head was oblong, not the round or wedge shape of most cats. And there was a flatness between the eyes. Also, the ears on these cats looked far too big for the head.

A century earlier, this strange kitten might have been drowned before anyone but the farm wife saw it, lest she be accused of witchcraft. However, this one was carefully tended and, when old enough, bred to his dam. She gave birth to another mixed litter, coated and hairless. Still more hairless kittens came with repeated matings and the breed was eventually established and registered.

By now, however, the name "hairless" no longer fits. By touch if not by look, a suede-soft downy layer is found on each foot and a bit of fuzzier down across the face, with almost-hairy tufts around the ears and more not-quite-hair on the body. At a glance, they still seemed hairless, but for honest naming the sponsors chose Sphynx, an old spelling. After all, the ancient Sphinx in Egypt's Valley of the Tombs was carved from rock and looks naked too.

Mutation rather than manipulation is involved in several other breeds. Among them is the Scottish Fold, whose turned-down ear tips give the furry head a baby-doll roundness sure to charm human hearts to protective fondness. Baby talk, however, is soon followed by utter amazement that this innocent is so cannily capable of looking after itself.

Mutation and miracle have both been given a role in creating the Birman breed. The French, however, are responsible for the name. To them, the Far East homeland of these longhaired cats with Siamese color points and four white paws is Birmanie, not Burma as it's spelled in English. And by a strange chance French fanciers were first to establish the breed in 1925.

A decade earlier a British army officer on duty in Burma/Birmanie saw these cats—a hundred of them, he thought—in the temple of Lao-Tsun and talked with the monks who cherished them as sacred. In olden times, they said, temple cats had been white. But one day, marauders seeking gold and jewels killed a priest as he worshiped beside the statue of a goddess famous for her gold-leaf body and sapphire eyes. They took their booty and ran, paying no heed to the cat who had come to give the dying priest last earthly comfort, each paw pressed against him with loving touch. The monks who found the two stared in wonder, for only the paws were white—the body now pale gold, dark brown on legs, tail and forehead, and almost-round eyes a gleaming sapphire blue. All temple cats had had these same fur colors, the same blue eyes ever since, they added.

The officer, Major Gordon Russell, might have forgotten both cats and story, but he was in charge of rescue when rebels attacked the temple and so on hand to help the priests and some of their cats escape to safety in Tibet. The grateful priests tried to find him after the war years, learned he had retired to France, and in 1919 they sent him a pair of their sacred cats. Russell, knowing proper action had to be taken or the breed might be lost, asked experienced French breeders to take charge. So the Birman breed was named and registered there in France in 1925, with acceptance coming from the British in 1966 and the States in 1967.

Since then designers have been adding other typical hues for Birman point colors by mating with Siamese of each accepted shade. But the long hair—medium length compared to Persians—has been the Birman's since temple days, no "designing" needed.

Perhaps success for round-eyed Birmans was the spark that set fanciers off on a search for longhaired cats with Siamese point colors and Persian eyes and body. Sweden may have been first with the pairings, but didn't carry through.

Breeders in England and the States worked separately and those in Germany and France together to produce three breeds that cannot easily be distinguished from each other. In the United States it's Himalayan, for England it's Colourpoint and in German and French it's Khmer (an old name for Cambodia). In 1950 another look-alike was accepted as a separate breed because of its habit of going completely limp at a touch—the name, Ragdoll.

All of this designer breeding has had one happy result for people who want a beautiful cat but not to breed or win at shows. Perfect cats by show standards may come rarely, perhaps only one to a litter, or none at all. Those that don't quite qualify may be sold at much lower prices as "pet quality" with all their love and loyalty and companionship still A-plus.

Some breeders seem to think only of achieving something different, welcoming even the reproduction of a blemish. Others at least have a goal. One who truly had a design in mind was Nikki Horner of Kentucky. Her dream was a pet of cat size as sleekly black as Kipling's Bagheera is pictured by readers who love his *Jungle Book*.

To get the sleek body she began with a dark brown female of the Burmese breed. Its own ancestors were a female from Burma and a Siamese male. She mated their daughter to a black short-hair, and the kittens that resulted were neither quite so black nor quite so sleek as she wanted.

So it was try again, and several more matings were needed before she was satisfied. Finally she thought she was as close as she could get and her new kittens were accepted for entry by the Cat Fanciers Association in 1976. The name she chose for them was Bombay, although neither she nor any of the cats or their ancestors had ever been there. However, it was accepted. For most people Bombay suggests India, where panthers as black as Bagheera can be found. Some other approved names lack even this roundabout geographical link.

The most expensive breeds are likely to be those most recently certified for registration, simply because there are fewer available. Among these is the Bengal, the offspring of a tabby crossed with a true wild species, the Leopard Cat, *Felis bengalensis*, native to Asia. Almost as wild looking is the Ocicat, the surprise result of a cross between Aby and Siamese. Why its face is so much like that of an ocelot, *Felis pardalis*, is just one of the mysteries that go with human interference in cat designing.

STILL HALF WILD, FATHERED BY A WILD ASIAN LEOPARD CAT, THERE'S LITTLE LIKENESS TO A TABBY MOTHER. MANY MORE LITTERS ARE AHEAD BEFORE A NEW TAME CAT BREED IS RECOGNIZED.

Klinger photo.

That mystery breed from Singapore, the Singapura, was considered a natural mutation at first. Its ticked coat, however, suggests *chaus* or Aby might have been involved, if not in the beginning then at least in recent efforts to improve a breed of uncertain origin.

Crossing established breeds is a custom that probably no one wants to stop. But introducing a half-wild breed may have dangers beyond control. Wildness isn't as easily lost as spots or stripes, as breeders who have crossed wolves with dogs have discovered. Does this hold for cats, too? That's only one of the questions troubling cat fanciers—and cat friends—these days.

14

ALWAYS QUESTIONS

When the questions are about cats, the answers are not always ready and waiting. Sometimes there isn't any indisputable answer already on file like sums and quotients in the back of the teacher's arithmetic book.

One that needs just such firm answer comes from members of the Cat Fancy and many others who enjoy going to cat shows and knowing each breed by name. Even for the experts, breed names are often confusing, especially at an international exhibit where familiar breeds do not have familiar names.

That's expected in foreign languages, but British breed names are sometimes different from those in the States. So the question needing an answer is this: How can breed names and other terminology be made the same, at least in all English-speaking countries? If that is accomplished, matching translations in other languages might be easily accepted.

Persuading British fanciers to accept other names may be difficult. Their officials were first to establish cat shows and terms and they have generally expected others to follow. Priority is the usual standard in scientific matters, so the feeling has some basis. However, some British terms don't transfer well.

For instance, "Foreign Shorthair" has been the term for long-bodied hybrids with solid-color coat even if bred in England; those with multicolored coat are "Oriental Shorthairs"—a puzzling distinction when both got their long bodies from a Siamese ancestor. Fanciers in the States have used "Oriental" for both since 1947. Over 150 color and pattern variations have so far been

THIS LONG-BODIED SHORTHAIR—A SIAMESE/TABBY CROSS—HISSES
AT SOME RIVAL PUSS TO PUSSH OFF.

Jenny Duchêne photo.

registered. Wouldn't records go more smoothly if both countries used the label "Long-bodied Shorthairs," adding color in parentheses if necessary?

Such a choice calls for a balancing description for a second category—Short-bodied Shorthairs—doesn't it? Any exhibit with enough entries to warrant further subdivisions could do so for that occasion, keeping *short* and *long* as their basic terms understood everywhere. Further descriptive terms with universally understood meaning could follow as necessary. In time, some groups might want to organize a show for natural breeds only, or just for designed breeds, or any other limited grouping defined with nonconfusing labels.

The decision to accept or reject any terms can be made only after discussion by those involved. Principal breeders in an area or officers of registries and similar bodies will want to hold conferences, debates. Will Colourpoint, for instance, win over Himalayan? Will Maltese replace Chartreux? Discussion is bound to be lengthy, and probably heated at times. Should priority of usage in print be the deciding factor, as it is for Latin labels? Or is there a better choice? The harmony of international terms seems worth consideration—and no small amount of effort.

SOUTH AMERICAN BREEDS DEVELOP

Two South American breeds may need new names and classification for another reason. These two, long considered well established as native wild species there, have always been unusually rare. In fact, they are so rare almost nothing is known of their habits. Even native tribal people do not seem to know much about them. And this suggests that perhaps they are not wildcats at all, but descendants of tame cats who took to the wilds for feral life so long ago—and in such isolated surroundings—that no record of their departure has survived.

That could have happened in South America's gold-mining areas any year from 1500 to 1800 when Europeans—especially Spaniards—were arriving by every ship, finding a fortune and racing off to spend it in more agreeable coastal climes or dying still with dreams of wealth unfulfilled. The first of these two feline puzzlers is the Pampas Cat, put on scientific record as *Felis colocolo* in 1810. Its fellow conundrum is the Mountain Cat *Felis jacobita* (Andean Mountain Cat on some lists) first recorded in 1875.

Both are not only rare but likely to become extinct. Both have been described as "like a house cat." Neither has been seen often enough in the wild so that the details of their daily life— courting, hunting, type of den—can be described in detail. Yet they have been sighted over a fairly wide range—the Mountain Cat only in the high Andes, but reported at least once in Peru, Bolivia, Chile and Argentina since 1875 discovery. The Pampas Cat has been seen most often in Argentina but also west to Chile and north to Ecuador. A pair was caught in the wild and lived in a zoo for several years, even had kittens.

The latest report is a fossil of what might be a Pampas Cat ancestor found in Argentina, but verifying its wild ancestry is as difficult as proving *Colocolo* descends from pets gone wild. One point for pet ancestry is their pattern of tabby stripes and bands rather than the rosettes of other South American small felids. Also, an enormous—and uncounted—number of cats came to these lands with Europeans. Fortunes changed suddenly for these families. They could be wiped out by disease, fire, flood, earthquake or rebellious workers. Joy or despair might bring a sudden urge to leave harsh mountain lands for the comfort and sunshine in coastal cities, and if the cats didn't come when called, they might have been left behind. Many a city cat today has had just such reasons for becoming a stray. If a mother and a male kit fled together—or brother and sister, or pregnant female—they would be able to start a feral band and might later be joined by others equally homeless. Some later mutation in marking would be expected.

Feral wandering could also have been started by cats suddenly turned into lone shipwreck castaways after coastal storms sent their owners' vessels crashing on the rocks. Many animals unused to swimming find themselves carried safely ashore by even the clumsiest paddle-paw splashing. Cats, their sharp claws ever ready, would be able to cling to any length of bobbing beam or plank tide-bound for shore. All up and down South American coasts shipwrecked farm animals did make shore safely and often along North American shores, too—shores that then were often deserted. Horses, pigs and cattle became lively Robinson Crusoes and have been recorded in many a letter home and colony history. Cats could surely have had the same adventure.

The name *pampas* indicates that a cat version of Crusoe with this label would have landed on the Atlantic's Argentine shores where these grassy plains stretch for miles. A cat named for the Andes arrived on the Pacific side where mountain peaks loomed beyond barren sandy desert all the way down from Ecuador to Magellan Strait. Greenery grows only where rivers flow down from mountain lakes and springs. People and settlements are only along the rivers, too. Native tribes on both coasts in lowlands or mountains would have considered any animal as flesh for food and the fur for clothes and bedding. On neither coast would weary, bedraggled cats be welcomed as pets. The catlike figures on pre-Columbian ceramics and metalware portray the largest, most feared predators—jaguar and puma—not cuddly pets. Their bared teeth are a fighter's challenge, not a friendly grin. Also, any abandoned pet would be frightened, difficult to reassure even if kindness were offered.

So, then, the theory that these two are survivors with tame-cat ancestry is worth considering. But the belief that at least the Pampas Cat is a native South American wildcat has support, too, from that long-buried fossil skeleton. Firm proof either way is difficult but the topic is still of interest these days when the ancestry of another possible shipwreck castaway on a small Japanese island is being argued.

A CAT FOR JAPAN?

How long this species has lived on the island of Iriomote is not certain. It was first reported by a Japanese naturalist exploring there in 1965 and recorded officially by other Japanese scientists two years later with the binomial *Mayailurus iriomotensis*. (The *may* could be from Latin *maius*, "old.") So far, this island,

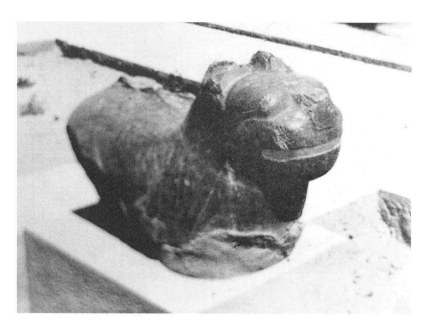

THIS COUGAR-PUMA-MOUNTAIN LION IN THE TIAHUANACO OPEN AIR MUSEUM IN LA PAZ, BOLIVIA, IS HISSING DEFIANCE, TOO. DON'T BE FOOLED IF YOU MEET A LIVE ONE.

Holmgren photo.

which belongs to Japan but is closer to Taiwan than to Tokyo, is the only place it has been seen. The Japanese, whose first tame cats were imported from China, have honored it as their only native wild felid and set aside a national reserve area for it on the island. The World Wildlife Fund has also been involved in its preservation, for some islanders continue to hunt it for food in spite of protective laws. The name, therefore, should be Iriomote Wildcat, not the current Iriomote Cat.

Other investigating naturalists prefer to list it as descending from a stranded Asian Leopard Cat, *Felis bengalensis,* native to the opposite mainland. They show somewhat similar markings and both are good swimmers. Storm winds and tides catching them feeding along the mainland coast could have set them adrift, and their own skill as swimmers would take them to island shores. No doubt DNA will be invoked to solve both these mysteries someday and prove whether the rare ones are native or emigrés from elsewhere.

WHAT IS A NATIVE?

Any question of native or nonnative cats brings reminder that some writers of cat lore seem confused by the word's meaning. One recent book on cats mistakenly declares that each cat is native to the place where it was born. A magazine writer, also in error, assures readers that domestic cats are native to Africa, Southern Europe and Western Asia and have probably been in America long enough to be called native here, too.

Dictionaries explain that *native* comes from Latin *nativus*, meaning "born." Eventually Europeans also used it for tribal people already living in the Americas and other far lands they explored, and it still has both meanings. Sometimes the phrase is *native-born* for clarity. Science, however, defines it differently when classifying plants and animals. A native wild species is one that first occurred in the area without human assistance, whether intentional or accidental. The dandelion, for all its abundance, is not a native American plant because it arrived here from the Old World on somebody's boots or in a chunk of garden soil. Domestic cat breeds, registered or not, are not native anywhere. They came into existence with considerable human help. Even mutant changes may need help to become fixed.

Perhaps this doesn't seem right. Foreign-born humans may become naturalized citizens by meeting certain requirements. So far, that privilege hasn't been extended to cats. They can be labeled American-born, British-born or whatever geographical label is appropriate if their birthplace is important. Adding "-born" distinguishes a factual label from those breed names that are fanciful concoctions devised for their romantic aura. Only the labels Angora, Persian, Siamese and a few others represent actual place of origin. Perhaps someday accurate labels will be required, but it doesn't seem likely.

Both tame cats and two of their wild ancestors were caught in this problem. The African Wildcat would be full species, but only for a time, as *Felis libyca libyca*. The Indian Desert Cat was quickly demoted to subspecies rank as *Felis libyca ornata*

SOFTER MORE KITTENLIKE WAYS MARK TODAY'S BENGALS, WHO HAVE HAD NO CONTACT WITH WILD ANCESTORS FOR MANY GENERATIONS.

Klinger photo.

or *Felis silvestris ornata* while the European Wildcat still remains a major species as *Felis silvestris silvestris.*

Few European or American readers protested. Most of them didn't know either of these two—did not know that *ornata* ranged from Egypt through Near East to Far East, was in no way a small isolated group that had broken away from the African.

They didn't know much about the African, either, for the next step turned both *libyca* and *ornata* into subspecies of the European *silvestris*. Of the three proven progenitors of the tame cat, only *chaus* stayed a full species. It is so different with its ticked coat that nobody would accept it as a subspecies of the European. The other two would be carelessly tagged *Felis silvestris* by writers who thought two Latin words enough; and because many readers recognized it only as the name for the European Wildcat, *ornata* and *libyca* were on their way to oblivion. *Ornata* was being omitted from many lists by 1965. *Libyca* took another two decades. In some recent books they both go unmentioned, even their territories marked as belonging to the European. One such map probably gave that magazine writer the idea that tame cats were native from England to India.

Realization of what was happening began to seep through. Readers who knew their cat history chanced on a few bald misstatements that set them shuddering. "Domestic cat history dates to the taming of the progenitor, *Felis silvestris,*" was one. Another: "*Silvestris*, direct ancestor of the domestic cat." That couldn't be! No way!

This Latin label belonged only to the European, and the European could *not* be ancestor of the m'yaow! How could it be when both ancient legends and recent reports from naturalists of note repeat that the European could not be tamed? Only *libyca, ornata* and *chaus* were in the right place at the right time to claim progenitor credit. The European Wildcat never got as far south as Egypt, where first taming in quantity took place. It didn't even have a chance to mate with a m'yaow and get its genes in the pool until Phoenician and Greek traders

THE MORE CATS YOU SEE TOGETHER, THE MORE YOU SEE THEM AS
INDIVIDUALS.

Sharbees photo.

began taking a *katta* or three to European ports and Roman
conquerors followed later with many a *catus*. Who could have
started such a wrong idea? Why?

The blame apparently goes to those who had been promoting
tagging *libyca* and *ornata* with *silvestris* two-part name (binomial) as a shortcut. Unwary readers hadn't realized, perhaps,
that the trinomial had to be used always or abandoned. As soon
as readers got the facts straight, more than a few began to
demand correction, usually meeting hothead refusal. Heat
increased with the suggestion that the changed labels were some
sort of finagling.

Some sort of finagling suggests itself with discovering that the
Felis catus label Linnaeus gave "the cat" on that famous 1758

LESSON I.

Words and Phrases to be learned by Sight only.

cat

a cat

the cat

my cat

the cat

a cat

LIKE MANY OTHER READERS, APPLETON'S FIRST READER OF *1878* BEGAN WITH "CAT" FOR THE FIRST LESSON—AND NOBODY ASKED, "WHAT'S THAT?"

list is being changed to *Felis silvestris catus*! If only a third word was wanting, *Felis catus catus* was the correct choice. So, then, was getting the European Wildcat on that 1758 list the spur behind all the changes in the Felidae listing?

The question has to be asked because a similar attempt was made over a century ago. Then the tactic was insisting that Linnaeus had meant his label for the European all along. Tame cats, the claimants insisted, should be entered as *Felis domesticus*. The choice seems logical, more meaningful.

Will similar influence—and plain facts—also restore the cat *felis catus* to rightful place and name beside *Canis familiaris*, the dog, and *Equus equus*, the horse? Will *libyca* and *ornata* regain the full rank they deserve and their place in the trio of tame cat progenitors? At present that is a wait-and-see affair.

Waiting also is involved with the need to give the English word *cat* and its equivalents in other languages back to the tame pets and homeless strays who have sole rights. Each member of a scientific family deserves a common name as well as Latin label. Among Felidae the tiger, lion and leopard, and several others, have always had their own names. Those still called *cat* should be relabeled *wildcat*. For double accuracy, *chaus* should change modifiers also, become Swamp Wildcat or Marsh Wildcat. *Ornata* is better described as Afro-Asian Wildcat. Or they might be given names used by humans in their native area. Several species already have native names.

Talking about a circus trainer's "cats" used to be an amusing bit of wordplay, or even a psychological ploy to calm a new trainer's reasonable concern for safety. Now c-a-t can no longer be the easiest word children learn to read and spell, always certain of its meaning. Any day they can open a magazine or book and see a tiger above the phrase "Big cat at play." The cougar pictured on a handsome collector's plate on grandmother's table is labeled "Canyon of the Cat." Will a cat-loving child reach out to pet the cougar she sees at the zoo? Or stop believing that grown-ups have "know best" rights?

Many questions about the cats that share our lives can be answered only by veterinarians and other professionals. Among others that keep nagging us for answers is how to find a new apartment, condominium or retirement center that welcomes cats. The dread alternatives of giving up a loved pet must be avoided—but how?

15
CATS IN OUR FUTURE

Among the difficult decisions that may keep nagging us for action is how to find a new apartment, condominium or retirement center that welcomes cats. The dread alternative of giving up a loved pet must be avoided. But how?

One way is to find a rental agent who will agree to locate a place that meets your other requirements and will accept cats, too. Usually even places that welcome cats have certain requirements to protect both owner and other occupants, and the cats themselves. The Massachusetts Society for the Prevention of Cruelty to Animals suggests that cat owners in search of new quarters ask the residents in a likely place to join them in offering the owner a petition to allow cats. Building owner and cat owner and fellow occupants all need protection from possible discomfort or property damage due to cats. Terms of agreement on such matters must be clearly stated.

Among other points of agreement must be having acceptable means of disposing of cat litter. Another usual agreement is that cats not be allowed to roam freely indoors or out, but be on leash outside their own quarters with collar or harness. A sturdy tree in a screened patio may help bring outdoor pleasures inside. Indoor perches appeal too.

Usually a harness is preferable, for it does not tighten to stranglehold if accidentally caught and held fast. A loose collar doesn't provide the restraint needed and may let the cat slip free when it needs to be held back for its own protection. But tug too hard at the leash of a frightened cat—even on a harness—and those

THE TREE DOESN'T HAVE TO BE GROWING IF IT CAN BE TIED OR NAILED DOWN FIRMLY SO IT WON'T TILT. ONLY A FEW CATS ARE TOO HEAVY FOR SUCH MAKE-DO.

Jenny Duchêne photo.

CATS STILL KNOW THE SAFETY RULES OF THE WILD: CLIMB HIGH OR BURROW DEEP.

Sharbees photo.

flexible shoulder joints that allow a cat to turn and twist in any direction without dislocating will work their magic. Off goes cat in a tumble—and maybe the owner as well.

A cat trained to be at ease in harness and leash under normal conditions will be able to enjoy far more than just a daily walk in the backyard or nearby park. It will also be prepared to accept the harness willingly for a trip to the veterinarian or a visit to cat-welcoming friends or whenever any emergency demanding prompt exit occurs. In going to and from an apartment, the cat in harness also allays the fears of nervous neighbors who happen to be ailurophobes and may wish they weren't.

Some older cats who have never been on leash may be difficult to train at first. Often taking them out to watch a mild-tempered cat who is already comfortable on leash will encourage them to submit. Even a familiar dog may set a good example. Praise and short first lessons help, too, along with ever-needed patience.

These days, one of the most serious questions challenging people who care about cats is what to do about "strays." The word seems to include every kind of wanderer: contented family cats accidentally separated from their people while traveling; cats terrified by sudden fire, flood, robbery or any other disaster, causing them to run far and maybe forget the way home; or unwanted cats that have been dumped in some out-of-the-way corner and abandoned. If they make it on their own for a while, and become truly feral, they may never be contented as a house cat again—especially if they're not allowed outdoors at all.

Indoor life is all but necessary for city cats these days. Freedom to roam has become an invitation to disaster from speeding cars. Sometimes cats who are only slightly wounded may be accepted by an animal shelter, but they may never be adopted. Some shelters have facilities for keeping abandoned cats till they die naturally, but others must resort to euthanasia after a few days.

Holmgren photo

Where does human responsibility lie? Many strays are sickly, infected with a disease they could spread to every animal or human they touch. Always hungry, they may kill not just mice and rats but many birds—even rare migrants bird-watchers value highly, as well as common sparrows or the blackbirds that flock in the hundreds and few humans welcome. Is trying to feed all cats who come to some convenient place where food can be provided daily by donors be right or wrong when their lives are so burdened with illness and lack of shelter? Can enough indoor space for homeless cats be found to make these outdoor feedings unnecessary?

More needed, perhaps, are measures that will make the number of strays diminish naturally. The Oregon Humane Society is among the many shelters already working toward this goal by marking the skin of each adopted stray with a permanent identification number so that owners can be notified if it is lost again. Could every city cat be required to have such ID mark as well as a license? Even more demanding, could all cat owners except licensed breeders be required to have their cats spayed or neutered? Such action may not be well received and the cost will not be small.

Other animals besides cats are abandoned and mistreated, of course. Dogs, horses, canaries, parakeets, rabbits, gerbils, hamsters all add to shelter costs. So do occasional goats and donkeys, turtles, lizards, raccoons, opossums—even snakes that have been housemates.

But cats in trouble are a special concern for people who have known the joy and wonder of a cat's companionship, loyalty and affection, and so the questions must be asked here in hope of answers. No need to ask if having a cat is worth the trouble. When the right cat and the right person get together, memories are treasure beyond counting.

INDEX